THE MILITARY HISTORICAL SOCIETY

SPECIAL NUMBER
1992

THE VOLUNTEER INFANTRY
1880 – 1908

by
Ray Westlake

Published by
The Military Historical Society
c/o The National Army Museum
Royal Hospital Road
Chelsea
London SW3 4HT

Copyright 1992
R.A. Westlake

All rights reserved. No part of this bnook may be reproduced or transmitted in copy form or by any means electronic or mechanical, including photocopying, recording for any information storage and retrieval system, without the permission of the Society and the Author.

ISBN 0 9510603 1 7

Printed in England by Signland Ltd, Farnham, Surrey GU9 9NN

ACKNOWLEDGEMENTS

I wish to record my thanks to the many members of the Military Historical Society who, over the past twenty years, have helped to provide the information which has made this publication possible. References relating to the Volunteers are scarce, but much of the material used has been produced by members of the Society.

I would also like to thank the staff of a number of museums and also private members who have helped with the photographs. Their names appear in the credits after the captions.

This project is a Society venture and I have involved as many of the members as possible. Finally, I would like to thank the staff of the Army Museums Ogilby Trust — Colonel Peter Walton and Major Alan Harfield (who have since retired) and Major John Tamplin, for providing not only access to the wealth of information held by the Trust, but also for their generous hospitality.

Dedication

To John Gaylor, Secretary of the Military Historical Society since 1965.

INTRODUCTION

The purpose of this work is to set out an "order of battle" for the volunteer infantry between 1880 and 1908. Each battalion has been listed under its regiment and where known the number and location of its companies has been recorded. The place-name given for a company is that of its headquarters. Generally, companies were concentrated in one city or town, but often a number of drill stations could exist outside of the main headquarters.

No attempt has been made here to go into any great detail regarding dress. The study of volunteer uniforms is complex, and due to the lack of published regulations probably more difficult than that of the Regular Army. What has been provided, however, is a simple record of the basic uniform colour and its facings.

Only the colours of full dress uniforms have been dealt with. Where scarlet is mentioned, it must be assumed that this is the colour of the tunic, the trousers being dark blue. All other colours would normally refer to the whole uniform.

Under the heading **Territorial Force** details have been given of new battalions formed in 1908. It must be noted, however, that the new formation is that to which most, or all, of the volunteer battalion transferred.

BRIEF HISTORY OF THE VOLUNTEER INFANTRY 1859-1908

The official birthday of the Volunteer Force is 12th May 1859, this being the date of the War Office's circular giving sanction for the formation of volunteer corps. Prior to this, however, a corps formed at Exeter in 1852 (later 1st Devonshire) and the Royal Victoria Rifles (later 1st Middlesex) were already in existence.

The initial response was tremendous and by the middle of 1860 many hundreds of corps ranging from half-companies to whole battalions had been raised. With this great number of independent formations it was soon realised by the Government that some form of higher organisation was necessary. Consequently the opportunity was given for smaller corps to amalgamate as one, or alternatively join a battalion for administrative purposes only.

Where amalgamation took place, the hitherto numbered and independent corps became companies of the new battalion. The administrative battalion, however, existed only for that purpose, its corps retaining their separate identities and independence. Between 1860 and 1880 administrative battalions, if desired, could consolidate as a single corps.

By General Regulations and Instructions dated 2nd July 1873, the United Kingdom was divided into seventy infantry sub-districts. Each was designated as a sub-district brigade, and to it were allotted for recruiting purposes, two line battalions and the militia and volunteers of a certain area. This was to be the first step towards the closer association of the volunteers with the regular forces.

In 1880 the recommendation of a committee set up to look into the organisation of the Volunteer Force — that all existing administrative battalions should consolidate — was carried out. Following the practice of previous consolidated battalions, the number of the senior corps in each was assumed. However, this led to gaps in the numbering of corps within counties, and in June a general renumbering from 1st onwards was ordered. Only one consolidated corps, the 6th Suffolk, retained its number, the county having just two battalions with numbers 1st and 6th. Subsequently, during the spring of 1880, more than one number was held by some corps. As this will undoubtedly lead to confusion, consolidated numbers given are those eventually assumed.

The infantry reorganisations of 1881 are well known — the old sub-districts being formed into territorial regiments with regular, militia and volunteer battalions. Whereas the regular and militia battalions of a regiment were numbered from 1st onwards, the volunteers were grouped in a separate sequence,

1

again from one forward.

Volunteer corps were not designated as volunteer battalions straight away, in fact some were never to assume the regiment's title and remained as numbered Rifle Volunteer Corps (from 1891 Volunteer Rifle Corps) until transfer to the Territorial Force. Those corps that did change appeared in General, later Army Orders with their new designation.

The higher organisation of the volunteer infantry into brigades commenced in 1888. Nineteen were created under Army Order 314 of July which were followed by a further twelve in September (Army Order 408). The number of battalions forming each brigade varied from just three in one case to seventeen in another. In 1890 (Army Orders 207 and 395) additional brigades were formed and the battalions distributed on a more even basis. The next change affecting volunteer infantry brigades occurred in 1906 when under Army Order 130 the total was brought up to forty-four.

In 1900, and under a Special Army Order dated 2nd January, volunteer battalions were called upon to raise companies for active service in South Africa. For each regular battalion serving in the war, one company was to be raised from its affiliated volunteers. These were to consist of 116 all ranks, who in order to surmount the difficulties of the Volunteer Act, had to enlist into the Regular Army for a period of one year.

Although each volunteer was permitted to wear the designation of his volunteer battalion or corps on the shoulder strap, companies as a whole were styled as numbered Volunteer Service Companies of their regiment. A separate organisation known as the City Imperial Volunteers was also formed within the London Metropolitan area.

Under the Territorial and Reserve Forces Act of 1907 the Volunteer Force ceased to exist on 31st March 1908 and on the following day the Territorial Force was born. The change was generally not a popular one with the volunteers, as the new system meant the reorganisation and in some cases, disbandment, of many of the existing companies. However, the new force was soon established and the majority of battalions were to transfer en bloc.

ROYAL SCOTS (LOTHIAN REGIMENT)

The Royal Scots was formed from the several units comprising Number 62 Sub-District; these were — 1st Regiment of Foot (1st and 2nd Battalions) the Edinburgh Light Infantry Militia (3rd Battalion) and the volunteers of Edinburgh, Berwickshire, Haddingtonshire, Linlithgowshire, Peeblesshire and Midlothian.

Queen's Rifle Volunteer Brigade.
"SOUTH AFRICA 1900-02"
Although never designated as such, the Queen's Rifle Volunteer Brigade served with the Royal Scots as its 1st, 2nd and 3rd Volunteer Battalions. Formed as the 1st Edinburgh (City) Rifle Volunteer Corps in 1859, the Brigade was divided into three battalions in 1888, total twenty-five companies. In 1900 two additional companies, one consisting of cyclists, were raised.

4th Volunteer Battalion. "SOUTH AFRICA 1901-02"
This battalion had its origins in a company of the 1st Edinburgh Rifle Volunteer Corps that consisted entirely of total abstainers. Founded by John Hope, a prominent member of the British Temperance League, Number 16 Company later provided the nucleus of a new corps of 'teetotallers', the 3rd Edinburgh. This was renumbered as 2nd in 1880. Shown as attached to the 1st Edinburgh Corps until 1888, the 2nd was that year redesignated as 4th Volunteer Battalion.

Originally six companies, the 4th Volunteer Battalion added an additional two in 1900 — one at Portobello and a second which was founded by members of the Church of Scotland Teachers' Training College. At the close of the Volunteer period there were 928 all ranks on the strength.

5th Volunteer Battalion. "SOUTH AFRICA 1900-02"
Originally the 1st Midlothian Rifle Volunteer Corps, which was formed at Leith in 1859 and became the 5th Volunteer Battalion, Royal Scots in 1888. Between 1880 and 1908 the establishment of the Battalion varied between ten and eleven companies, most of which were recruited at Leith.

6th Volunteer Battalion. "SOUTH AFRICA 1901"
The 6th Volunteer Battalion was recruited both in Midlothian and Peeblesshire and was, prior to 1888, the 2nd Midlothian Rifle Volunteer Corps. This corps had been formed in 1880 by the consolidation of the 1st Admin. Battalion of Midlothian Rifle Volunteers and was designated as 6th Volunteer Battalion in 1888. Battalion headquarters moved from Penicuik to Peebles in 1907 and the original company locations were — Dalkeith (4), Penicuik, Valleyfield, Musselburgh, Loanhead,

Peebles (2) and Inverleithen. In 1895 one of the Dalkeith companies, 'D', was moved to Bonnyrigg.

7th Volunteer Battalion. "SOUTH AFRICA 1901"
This battalion was from Haddington where in 1860 the 1st Admin. Battalion of Haddingtonshire Rifle Volunteers was formed. In 1880 the Battalion was consolidated as 1st Corps, this in turn being designated as 7th Volunteer Battalion in 1888. Battalion establishment was six companies originally located — Haddington (2), Aberlady, East Linton, West Barns and North Berwick. During 1880 the personnel at West Barns ('E' Company) were absorbed into 'D' at East Linton. A new 'E' was then formed at Prestonpans and in 1906 part of this company was used to form a new 'C', the former 'C' Company at Aberlady having been absorbed into 'A' at Haddington. The strength of the Battalion just prior to transfer to the Territorial Force in 1908 was 994 all ranks.

8th Volunteer Battalion. "SOUTH AFRICA 1901-02"
In 1880 the several rifle corps then in existence within the County of Linlithgowshire (six formed between 1860-1878) were amalgamated to form one corps numbered as 1st. Upon joining the Royal Scots the 1st Linlithgowshire Rifle Volunteer Corps comprised headquarters at Linlithgow and seven companies — Linlithgow, Bo'ness, Torphichen, Bathgate, Uphall, Addiewell and West Calder. In 1881 the Torphichen Company ('C') was moved to Armadale and in 1888 the Corps became 8th Volunteer Battalion. An increase in establishment was sanctioned in 1900, two new companies being added to the Battalion at South Queensferry (disbanded in 1906) and Kirkliston. Also that year 'F' Company (Addiewell) moved to Fauldhouse.

9th Volunteer Battalion (Highlanders). "SOUTH AFRICA 1901-02"
In 1900 a number of Highlanders then living in Edinburgh decided to form a kilted battalion from within the city. Subsequently the Highland Battalion, Queen's Rifle Volunteer Brigade was formed with eight companies. The following year it was constituted as an independent unit and from then on served as 9th Volunteer Battalion. The last strength returns issued by the Battalion recorded 734 all ranks.

1st Berwickshire Rifle Volunteer Corps
This corps served as a volunteer battalion of the Royal Scots until 1887, when it was transferred to the King's Own Scottish Borderers.

1. Surgeon-Lieutenant Colonel Charles James Allan VD, Medical Officer 6th Volunteer Battalion, The Royal Scots c1896. (Army Museums Ogilby Trust).

Uniform

Scarlet was worn by the 4th, 5th and 6th Volunteer Battalions, the 4th having blue facings while the 5th and 6th had black. After 1888 sanction was given for these battalions to adopt the full uniform of the Royal Scots, Sutherland tartan trews being retained by the rank and file of the 4th and 5th Volunteer Battalions until 1908. The Queen's Rifle Volunteer Brigade had a dark grey uniform and both the 7th and 8th wore green with scarlet facings. Hunting Stewart trews with drab doublets were worn by the 7th Volunteer Battalion after 1904. In the 9th Volunteer Battalion scarlet doublets with blue facings were worn with kilts of Hunting Stewart tartan.

Territorial Force

In 1908 all units became Territorial battalions of the Royal Scots, the Queen's Rifle Volunteer Brigade forming the 4th and 5th, 4th Volunteer Battalion the 6th, 5th Volunteer Battalion the 7th, 6th and 7th Volunteer Battalions the 8th, 8th Volunteer Battalion the 10th (Cyclist) and 9th Volunteer Battalion the 9th (Highlanders).

QUEEN'S (ROYAL WEST SURREY REGIMENT)

The Regiment's regular and militia battalions were provided by the various battalions comprising Number 48 Sub-District: 2nd Regiment of Foot (1st and 2nd Battalions) and the 2nd Royal Surrey Militia (3rd Battalion). Also part of the same brigade were four Surrey volunteer corps, all these being redesignated as volunteer battalions of the Regiment in 1883.

1st Volunteer Battalion. "SOUTH AFRICA 1900-02"
The Battalion was formed as the 2nd Surrey Rifle Volunteer Corps at Croydon in 1859, and by 1880 comprised six companies located at Croydon, Crystal Palace and Caterham. Later, additional personnel were sanctioned to bring the establishment up to ten companies, but one of these was lost in 1903. According to the Battalion's last return, made in 1907, its total enrolled strength stood at 599 all ranks. At this time the nine companies were located — Croydon (7) Crystal Palace and Caterham.

2. 2nd Lieutenant C.E. Jefferis, 1st Volunteer Battalion, Queen's (Royal West Surrey Regiment) 1905. (Army Museums Ogilby Trust).

2nd Volunteer Battalion. "SOUTH AFRICA 1900-02"
The 2nd Volunteer Battalion was formerlly the 4th Surrey Rifle Volunteer Corps, and prior to that, the 3rd Admin. Battalion of Surrey Rifle Volunteers. Its senior company was formed as 5th Surrey Rifle Volunteer Corps in 1859, and in 1880 this number was used for a few months by the consolidated 3rd Admin. Battalion.

In 1880 the 4th Surrey comprised six companies — Reigate (2), Guildford (3) and Farnham; three additional companies being sanctioned before 1908. Headquarters were originally placed at Dorking, but in 1881 a move was made to Reigate, and then ten years later new premises were found in Guildford. The last return of the Battalion, made in 1907, gave a strength of 838 all ranks.

3rd Volunteer Battalion. "SOUTH AFRICA 1900-02"
In 1868 two Surrey rifle corps dating from 1860/61 — the 10th and 23rd, were placed together as the 4th Admin. Battalion of Surrey Rifle Volunteers. These two units were subsequently amalgamated as 6th Corps in 1880.

The original establishment of the Battalion, and that existing in 1908, was eight companies — Bermondsey (2) and Rotherhithe (6). Headquarters were in South East London at Jamaica Road, Bermondsey. A total enrolled strength of 596 all ranks was returned in 1907.

4th Volunteer Battalion. "SOUTH AFRICA 1900-02"
This battalion was formed as the 19th Surrey Rifle Volunteer Corps at Lambeth in 1860 and renumbered as 8th in 1880. With its headquarters in South East London: New Street, Kennington Park, the Battalion in 1881 comprised eight companies. Two more were sanctioned in 1890, and in 1900 the formation of a cyclist company was approved by the War Office. The Battalion's last return, made in 1907, recorded a total enrolled strength of 1,189.

Uniform
Three volunteer battalions of the Regiment wore green uniforms with scarlet facings. One, the 3rd, had scarlet with blue.

Territorial Force
In 1908 the 1st and 2nd Volunteer Battalions transferred to the Territorial Force as the 4th and 5th Queen's respectively. At the same time the 3rd Volunteer Battalion became the 22nd London Regiment while the 4th provided that regiment's 24th Battalion.

BUFFS (EAST KENT REGIMENT)

The several battalions comprising Number 45 Sub-District in 1881 formed the East Kent Regiment — 1st and 2nd Battalions (late 3rd Foot), 3rd and 4th Battalions (late East Kent Militia) and the 2nd and 5th Kent Rifle Volunteer Corps which assumed their volunteer battalion titles in 1883.

1st Volunteer Battalion. "SOUTH AFRICA 1900-02"
In 1874 the several companies comprising the 4th Administrative Battalion of Kent Rifle Volunteers were amalgamated with those of the 2nd Cinque Ports Administrative Battalion under the title of 5th Kent Rifle Volunteer Corps. This number was changed to 2nd in 1880. The majority dating from 1859/60, the ten original companies of the Battalion were located at — Ramsgate, Canterbury (2), Hythe, Sittingbourne, Margate, Ashford, Wingham, Dover and New Romney. Battalion headquarters moved from Canterbury to Dover in 1901. In 1893 "L" Company at New Romney was transferred to Lydd and three years later "D" at Hythe went to Folkstone. During the Boer War additional personnel were raised at Westgate-on-Sea, Herne Bay. Birchington, Broadstairs, Canterbury and Dover bringing the Battalion's establishment up to sixteen companies, two being cyclist formations. A reduction in strength to twelve companies was made in 1905, those listed in 1907 being — Ramsgate, Canterbury, Birchington, Folkestone, Sittingbourne, Herne Bay, Margate, Ashford, Wingham, Dover, Lydd and one Cyclist.

2nd (the Weald of Kent) Volunteer Battalion. "SOUTH AFRICA 1900-02"
In 1880 the 5th Administrative Battalion of Kent Rifle Volunteers was consolidated under the title of its senior company, the 37th Kent. This corps, which was renumbered as 5th within a few months, had its headquarters at Cranbrook and comprised seven companies — Cranbrook, Hawkhurst, Staplehurst, Lamberhurst, Brenchley, Rolvenden and Tenterden.

Uniform
Both battalions wore green uniforms, the 1st having scarlet facings.

Territorial Force
In 1908 the 4th and 5th Battalion of the Buffs were formed by the 1st and 2nd Volunteer Battalions respectively.

3. 1st Volunteer Battalion, Buffs (East Kent Regiment) c1904.

KING'S OWN
(ROYAL LANCASTER REGIMENT)

Prior to 1881 Number 11 Sub-District comprised the two battalions of the 4th Regiment of Foot, the 1st Royal Lancashire Militia, also two battalions, and the 10th Lancashire Rifle Volunteer Corps. Subsequently, in 1881, these regiments became the King's Own.

1st Volunteer Battalion. "SOUTH AFRICA 1900-02"
In 1861 the 5th Administrative Battalion of Lancashire Rifle Volunteers was formed at Ulverston comprising 37A, 37B, 37C, 52nd and 53rd Lancashire Corps. Several other companies that had been raised during 1859/60 later joined, including one from the school at Rossall. Consolidated in 1876 as the 10th Lancashire Rifle Volunteer Corps, the Battalion subsequently became the 1st Volunteer Battalion, King's Own in 1883.

Headquarters of the new corps remained at Ulverston and its nine companies were located at Lancaster (2), Ulverston (2), Barrow (2), Hawkshead, Rossall and Grange. In 1887 two new companies were formed at Dalton, but in 1889 the headquarters of one of these was moved to Millom. The Rossall Company was disbanded in 1890.

In 1900 it was decided to split the battalion and form a 2nd for the Regiment. This was achieved by the transfer of personnel from the original battalion leaving the 1st with eight companies — Ulverston (2), Barrow (3), Hawkshead, Dalton and Millom.

2nd Volunteer Battalion. "SOUTH AFRICA 1900-02"
The 2nd Volunteer Battalion was formed in 1900 from members of the 1st. Headquarters were placed in Lancaster and the six company establishment was located — Lancaster (4), Morecambe and Grange.

Uniform
Scarlet tunics with blue facings were adopted by the 5th Admin. Battalion in 1863 and worn by both battalions through to 1908.

Territorial Force
In 1908 the 1st and 2nd Volunteer Battalions provided the Regiment's two Territorial battalions, 4th and 5th.

4. F Company, 1st Volunteer Battalion King's Own (Royal Lancaster Regiment). Winning team — Tilney Challenge Cup 1894. (King's Own Regimental Museum)

NORTHUMBERLAND FUSILIERS

The County of Northumberland provided the Battalions for Number 1 Sub-District and subsequently, in 1881, formed the Northumberland Fusiliers — 1st and 2nd Battalions (late 5th Foot) and 3rd Battalion (late Northumberland Militia). The two rifle volunteer corps from the County, together with that from Newcastle-upon-Tyne, provided the Regiment's volunteer battalions, redesignation taking place in 1883.

1st Volunteer Battalion. "SOUTH AFRICA 1900-02"
The 1st Administrative Battalion of Northumberland Rifle Volunteers was consolidated as the 1st Northumberland and Berwick-upon-Tweed Rifle Volunteer Corps in 1880; most of its companies dating from 1859/60. At this time headquarters was located at Alnwick (moving to Hexham in 1891) and the ten company establishment — Hexham, Morpeth, Belford, Alnwick, Bellingham, Allendale, Berwick, Lowick, Corbridge and Haltwhistle. In 1885 the Lowick Company ("H") was disbanded and replaced by one at Newburn. Nine years later the Newburn personnel were transferred to the 2nd Volunteer Battalion and at the same time yet another "H" Company was formed, this time at Prudhoe.

In 1900 two additional companies were sanctioned bringing the establishment of the Battalion up to twelve. By this time certain reorganisations had taken place and company locations were - Hexham (2), Belford, Alnwick, Bellingham, Haydon Bridge, Berwick, Prudhoe, Corbridge, Haltwhistle and Morpeth (2). The two Hexham Companies ("A" and "B") were merged in 1903, a replacement "B" being found by the transfer of No.7 Company, 2nd Northumberland Royal Garrison Artillery (Vols) at Ashington. The Battalion's strength was returned as 1,372 all ranks, just twenty short of establishment, in 1907.

2nd Volunteer Battalion. "SOUTH AFRICA 1900-02"
The 8th Northumberland Rifle Volunteer Corps was formed out of the 1st Corps in 1861. This in turn became 2nd Corps in 1880 and as a volunteer battalion of the Northumberland Fusiliers originally comprised Headquarters and six companies, all at Walker. In 1894 the Newburn Company of the 1st Volunteer Battalion was transferred to the 2nd as "G" Company. The following year "H" at Wallsend was formed and in 1900 additional companies were sanctioned bringing the establishment up to ten. With the inclusion of new personnel, and a number of company relocations, the companies of the 2nd Volunteer Battalion in 1900 were organised — Walker (4), Newburn (2), Wallsend (2) and Gosforth (2). Some 896 all ranks were recorded in the Battalion's last return.

3rd Volunteer Battalion. "SOUTH AFRICA 1900-02"
Headquarters of the 3rd Volunteer Battalion were in Newcastle, where in 1860 the 1st Newcastle-upon-Tyne Rifle Volunteer Corps was formed out of the Newcastle Rifle Club. In 1881 the establishment of the Battalion stood at eight companies, all of these being located at headquarters — St George's Drill Hall, St. Mary's Place. During the Boer War two additional companies were sanctioned, one being raised by the clerks of various banks and quayside offices, and the other by members of Durham University.

Uniform
The 1st Volunteer Battalion wore grey uniforms with scarlet facings, the 2nd, scarlet with green facings and the 3rd scarlet with black, changing to white facings in 1886.

Territorial Force
In 1908 the 1st Volunteer Battalion provided the 4th and part of the 7th Battalions, Northumberland Fusiliers. At the same time the 2nd and 3rd transferred as 5th and 6th Battalions respectively.

5. Other ranks glengarry badge 1885-1895 1st Volunteer Battalion, Northumberland Fusiliers. (Denis Wood)

ROYAL WARWICKSHIRE REGIMENT

Prior to the 1881 reorganisation, the County of Warwickshire provided the several units comprising Number 28 Sub-District, there being six battalions, two each for the Line, Militia and Volunteers. In 1881 the Royal Warwickshire Regiment was formed — 1st and 2nd Battalions (late 6th Foot), 3rd and 4th Battalions (late 1st and 2nd Warwick Militia) and the 1st and 2nd Warwickshire Rifle Volunteer Corps.

1st Volunteer Battalion. "SOUTH AFRICA 1900-02"
Headquarters of the Battalion were in Birmingham where its original company was formed as the 1st Warwickshire Rifle Volunteer Corps in 1859. The strength of the Corps soon reached twelve companies, an establishment that was maintained up till redesignation as 1st Volunteer Battalion in 1883. Subsequently, in 1891, an additional four companies were sanctioned and the Battalion was constituted as a "double battalion." The strength was again increased in 1900 when the Cyclist Section was made up to a full company and a new company was created at Birmingham University.

2nd Volunteer Battalion. "SOUTH AFRICA 1900-02"
In 1860 all Warwickshire rifle corps, and any subsequently formed, outside of Birmingham were organised into an administrative battalion. The first of these companies had been raised in 1859 and in 1880 all units were merged as the 2nd Warwickshire Rifle Volunteer Corps. With headquarters at Coventry the twelve companies of the new battalion were located — Coventry (4), Rugby (2), Warwick, Stratford-on-Avon, Nuneaton, Saltley and Leamington (2). Redesignation as 2nd Volunteer Battalion was in 1883.

In 1900 an additional company was sanctioned, but by the end of the following year the establishment of the Battalion had been reduced down to eleven companies.

Uniform
According to the Regimental history of the Battalion, the uniform of the "60th Rifles" (green/scarlet) was introduced in 1863 to replace the grey and green hitherto worn. The Regiment's scarlet/blue was adopted by the 1st Admin. Battalion prior to 1881, and this was maintained up till 1908 by the 2nd Volunteer Battalion.

Territorial Force
In 1908 the 1st Volunteer Battalion provided the Regiment's 5th and 6th Battalions (TF), and from the students' company, the Birmingham University O.T.C. The 2nd formed the 7th (TF).

6. Colonel W. Swynfen Jervis, Commanding Officer 1st Volunteer Battalion, Royal Warwickshire Regiment 1882-1900.

ROYAL FUSILIERS
(CITY OF LONDON REGIMENT)

The Royal Fusiliers was recruited in the Metropolitan area and in 1881 comprised 1st and 2nd Battalions (late 7th Foot), 3rd, 4th and 5th Battalions (late Royal Westminster, Royal London, Royal South Middlesex Regiments of Militia) and four Middlesex volunteer corps.

5th Middlesex (West Middlesex) Rifle Volunteer Corps
This Corps was allotted to the Royal Fusiliers in 1881 and together with the 9th Middlesex Rifle Volunteers formed one of its volunteer battalions. Both corps were transferred to the King's Royal Rifle Corps in 1883.

9th Middlesex Rifle Volunteer Corps
Formed a volunteer battalion with the 5th Middlesex Rifle Volunteer Corps until 1883 when both corps were transferred to the King's Royal Rifle Corps.

22nd Middlesex (Central London Rangers) Rifle Volunteer Corps
Served as a volunteer battalion of the Royal Fusiliers until transferring to the King's Royal Rifle Corps in 1882.

1st Volunteer Battalion. "SOUTH AFRICA 1900-02"
This battalion was formed in 1859 as the 19th Middlesex Rifle Volunteer Corps by members of the Working Men's College at Bloomsbury in London. Renumbered as 10th in 1880 the Battalion served as part of the King's Royal Rifle Corps until 1883 when it joined the Royal Fusiliers as its 1st Volunteer Battalion. Upon joining the Regiment, headquarters of the Battalion was situated at No.33 Fitzroy Square in West London and there were ten companies (eleven from 1900) located around the Metropolitan area.

2nd Volunteer Battalion. "SOUTH AFRICA 1900-02"
Formed in 1861 as the 46th Middlesex Rifle Volunteer Corps this battalion was redesignated as 23rd Corps in 1880 and then as 2nd Volunteer Battalion, Royal Fusiliers in 1883. Headquarters were at 9 Tufton Street, Westminster and the Battalion's establishment was eight companies.

3rd Volunteer Battalion. "SOUTH AFRICA 1900-02"
The 3rd Volunteer Battalion dates from 1859 when it was formed in Euston, London as the 20th Middlesex Rifle Volunteer Corps. Much of the Corps was found from workers of the London and North Western Railway Company and in 1880

this connection was recognised when a new title was assumed — 11th Middlesex (Railway). It was not until 1890 that the 11th Middlesex joined the Regiment as its 3rd Volunteer Battalion, it having served with both the King's Royal Rifle Corps and Middlesex Regiment prior to this. Additional personnel were sanctioned during 1900/01, increasing the establishment from eight to thirteen companies, but a reduction to eleven was made after the Boer War.

4th Volunteer Battalion. "SOUTH AFRICA 1900"
The origins of this battalion lay in several rifle corps that were formed in the Tower Hamlets area of London during 1860. In 1868 two corps, the 2nd and 4th, were amalgamated as 1st, and then, in 1874, the 6th Corps also joined. The 1st, or Tower Hamlets Rifle Volunteer Brigade, until 1904 served as a volunteer battalion of the Rifle Brigade. It transferred to the Royal Fusiliers in May of that year and at the same time assumed the 4th Volunteer Battalion designation. Headquarters of the Battalion were at 112 Shaftesbury Street and its strength stood at eleven companies.

Uniform
All battalions wore scarlet with blue facings.

Territorial Force
The four battalions all became part of the London Regiment in 1908, forming the 1st to 4th Battalions in order of seniority.

7. Officers cap 1st Volunteer Battalion, Royal Fusiliers. (National Army Museum)

KING'S (LIVERPOOL REGIMENT)

The King's (Liverpool Regiment) was formed out of the several battalions that comprised Number 13 Sub-District Brigade in 1881 — 1st and 2nd Battalions (late 8th Foot), 3rd and 4th Battalions (late 2nd Royal Lancashire Militia). Volunteer corps were — 1st, 5th, 13th, 15th, 18th and 19th Lancashire and the 1st Isle of Man. These were all designated as volunteer battalions in 1888.

1st Volunteer Battalion. "SOUTH AFRICA 1900-02"
In 1860 the 1st Lancashire Rifle Volunteer Corps, raised in the previous year, was merged with a number of other independent companies from the Liverpool area. With a strength of ten companies, the 1st Corps became a volunteer battalion of the King's Regiment in 1881 and by 1883 an additional two companies had been sanctioned and formed. Another company was raised in 1900.

2nd Volunteer Battalion. "SOUTH AFRICA 1900-01"
In 1862 part of the 2nd Administrative Battalion of Lancashire Rifle Volunteers, together with a number of other corps raised since 1859, was amalgamated as the Liverpool Rifle Volunteer Brigade, or 5th Corps. The Battalion joined the King's Regiment with a strength of ten companies in 1881 and maintained this establishment up to 1908.

3rd Volunteer Battalion. "SOUTH AFRICA 1900-02"
The Regiment's 3rd Volunteer Battalion originated from two Lancashire rifle volunteer corps — the 13th, formed at Southport in 1859, and the 54th, formed the following year at Ormskirk. Amalgamated as 13th Corps in 1880, the Battalion comprised headquarters at Southport and six companies — four in Southport and two in Ormskirk. Two additional companies were sanctioned in 1899, the personnel being found out of the Cyclist and Mounted Infantry sections. The Battalion was disbanded in 1908.

4th Volunteer Battalion. "SOUTH AFRICA 1900-02"
The 15th Lancashire Rifle Volunteer Corps was formed in Liverpool in 1860 and joined the King's Regiment in 1881 with an establishment of ten companies, three, according to the Historical Records of the King's, being in Bootle. An extra company was raised as a result of the increase in volunteers during the Boer War.

**5th (Irish) Volunteer Battalion.
"SOUTH AFRICA 1900-02"**
Formed in 1860 as the 64th Lancashire Rifle Volunteer Corps,

19

8. Officer 8th (Scottish) Volunteer Battalion King's (Liverpool Regiment) 1908.
(Army Museums Ogilby Trust)

the "Liverpool Irish" were renumbered as 18th Corps in 1880 and provided six companies as the Regiment's 5th Volunteer Battalion. In 1900 two additional companies were sanctioned, but five years later one of these was disbanded and replaced by a Cyclist company.

6th Volunteer Battalion. "SOUTH AFRICA 1900-01"
This battalion originated in 1860 when some 473 members of the newspaper and printing trade in Liverpool offered their services as a volunteer corps. Subsequently the 80th Lancashire (Liverpool Press Guard) was formed. This was renumbered as 19th Corps in 1880, and in the following year provided the Regiment's 6th Volunteer Battalion. The original strength of the Battalion was eight companies, one extra (cyclists) being added in 1902. By the end of 1907, however, one company had been disbanded.

7th (Isle of Man) Volunteer Battalion
By 1880 only one rifle volunteer corps from the Isle of Man remained in existence. This was the 2nd, formed at Douglas in 1860, which in 1880 was renumbered as 1st. With a strength of just one company, the 7th was attached to the 6th Volunteer Battalion.

When the Territorial Force was created in 1908 the Isle of Man Volunteers did not transfer. Instead they remained in the Army List as 7th (Isle of Man) Volunteer Battalion, The King's (Liverpool Regiment), and as such continued to serve under the old volunteer system. The Battalion was to hold the unique distinction of being the only volunteer unit until 1914 and the introduction of the Volunteer Training Corps.

8th (Scottish) Volunteer Battalion. "SOUTH AFRICA 1900-02"
This battalion (eight companies) was formed in 1900 from Scots resident in the City of Liverpool.

Uniform
The uniforms of the battalions were — 1st (Green with black facings), 2nd (green/scarlet), 3rd (scarlet/blue), 4th (scarlet/blue), 5th (green/scarlet, plain green by 1904), 6th (scarlet/blue), 7th (scarlet/blue) and 8th (drab/red).

Territorial Force
The Regiment's six Territorial battalions (5th to 10th) were formed by the 1st, 2nd, 4th, 5th, 6th and 8th Volunteer Battalions respectively.

NORFOLK REGIMENT

The Norfolk Regiment was formed in 1881 out of the several units comprising Number 31 Sub-District Brigade — 1st and 2nd Battalions (late 9th Foot), 3rd Battalion (late 1st or West Norfolk Militia), 4th Battalion (late 2nd or East Norfolk Militia) and the 1st to 4th Norfolk Rifle Volunteer Corps. The latter assumed the title of the Regiment in 1883.

1st Volunteer Battalion. "SOUTH AFRICA 1900-02"
The senior volunteer corps of the County of Norfolk was formed at Norwich in 1859 and until 1883 was known as the 1st Norfolk (City of Norwich) Rifle Volunteer Corps. The strength of the Battalion was six companies.

2nd Volunteer Battalion. "SOUTH AFRICA 1900-02"
The 2nd Volunteer Battalion was previously the 2nd Norfolk Rifle Volunteer Corps and before that the County's 1st Administrative Bn. With headquarters at Great Yarmouth the Battalion was recruited in both Norfolk and Suffolk, its original nine companies (a tenth was formed in 1885) being located at Great Yarmouth (4), Gorleston, Bungay, Beccles and Lowestoft (2).

3rd Volunteer Battalion. "SOUTH AFRICA 1900-02"
In 1872 the 3rd Norfolk Rifle Volunteer Corps was formed out of the County's original 1st Administrative Battalion (a new 1st Admin. was formed in 1877 and subsequently became 2nd Corps in 1880). Headquarters of the Battalion were at East Dereham and its ten company strength originally located at King's Lynn, Aylsham, Holkham, Reepham, East Dereham, Swaffham, Heacham, Holt, Downham Market and North Walsham.

4th Volunteer Battalion. "SOUTH AFRICA 1900-02"
Headquarters of the 4th Volunteer Battalion were in Norwich, the Battalion being previously the 4th Norfolk Rifle Volunteer Corps and before that the County's 2nd Administrative Bn. At the formation of the 4th Corps in 1872, seven and a half companies — Harleston, Diss (½), Loddon, Stalham, Blofield, Attleborough, Wymondham and Thetford were condensed into six. These, in 1899, were located at Harleston, Diss, Loddon, Stalham, Blofield and Attleborough. Establishment was increased from six to ten companies in 1900.

Uniform
All four battalions wore scarlet uniforms with white facings, the 4th changing from grey in 1888.

Territorial Force

In 1908 the 1st and 4th Volunteer Battalions were merged as 4th Bn. (TF) while the 2nd and 3rd provided the Regiment's 5th Bn. (TF).

9. Bandsmen from the East Lynn Company, 3rd Volunteer Battalion, Norfolk Regiment, going to camp in July, 1906.

LINCOLNSHIRE REGIMENT

The Lincolnshire Regiment was created in 1881 out of the battalions then comprising Number 30 Sub-District Brigade — 1st and 2nd Battalions (late 10th Foot), 3rd Battalion (late Royal North Lincoln Militia) and 4th Battalion (late Royal South Lincoln Militia). The volunteers were provided by the 1st and 2nd Lincolnshire Corps, and these were designated as volunteer battalions in 1883.

1st Volunteer Battalion. "SOUTH AFRICA 1900-02"
The 1st Volunteer Battalion was formerlly the 1st Administrative Battalion. The Battalion's original eleven companies all dated from 1859/60 and were located at Lincoln (3), Louth, Great Grimsby, Spilsby, Horncastle, Alford, Barton, Gainsborough and Market Rasen which moved to Frodingham in 1881. Headquarters were in Lincoln.

In 1900 a number of companies were detached to form the Regiment's 3rd Volunteer Battalion, the 1st then being reorganised as follows:- Headquarters and four companies at Lincoln, two at Gainsborough and one at Horncastle.

2nd Volunteer Battalion. "SOUTH AFRICA 1900-02"
Grantham was the headquarters of the 2nd Volunteer Battalion; until 1883 the 2nd Lincolnshire Rifle Volunteer Corps, and between 1860-80, the 2nd Administrative Battalion of Lincolnshire Rifle Volunteers. The Battalion's eight companies were, in 1881, located at Grantham (2), Boston, Stamford, Sleaford, Spalding, Gosberton and Billingborough.

3rd Volunteer Battalion. "SOUTH AFRICA 1900-02"
The 3rd Volunteer Battalion was formed in June, 1900 by withdrawing the Louth, Grimsby, Spilsby, Alford, Barton and Frodingham Companies from the 1st Volunteer Battalion. Headquarters were at Grimsby and the Battalion's establishment was set at eight companies.

Uniform
In 1881 the uniform of the 1st Volunteer Battalion was scarlet, its yellow facings being changed for white by 1885. In the 2nd, scarlet with blue facings was worn and from its formation in 1900, the 3rd wore scarlet and white.

Territorial Force
Upon transfer to the Territorial Force in 1908, the three battalions were merged to form the Regiment's 4th and 5th Battalions (TF).

10. Lt-Col. J.G. Williams, VD, Commanding Officer 1st Volunteer Battalion, Lincolnshire Regiment 1894-1901.

DEVONSHIRE REGIMENT

In 1881 the several battalions comprising Number 34 Sub-District Brigade became the Devonshire Regiment. With two line, two militia and five volunteer battalions, the Regiment was organised as follows:- 1st and 2nd Battalions (late 11th Foot), 3rd Battalion (late 2nd Devon Militia), 4th Battalion (late 1st Devon Militia) and the 1st to 5th Devonshire Rifle Volunteer Corps. The latter received the title of the Regiment in 1885.

1st (Exeter and South Devon) Volunteer Battalion. "SOUTH AFRICA 1900-01"

The 1st Devonshire Rifle Volunteer Corps was the senior volunteer unit in the United Kingdom, it being the first to be officially recognised by the Government. It was in 1852 that the services of the Exeter and South Devon Rifle Corps were offered to the War Office. The unit was accepted and on 4 January, 1853 Her Majesty Queen Victoria signed the commissions of the Corps first officers.

Numbered as 1st Corps in 1859, the Battalion originally contained eleven companies, a reduction to ten was made during 1892, and these were located in addition to Exeter at Exmouth, Credition, Dawlish and Teignmouth.

2nd (Prince of Wales's) Volunteer Battalion. "SOUTH AFRICA 1900-01"

The 2nd Administrative. Battalion of Devonshire Rifle Volunteers was formed in 1860 comprising a number of corps that had been formed during 1859/60. In 1880 consolidation as 2nd Devonshire R.V.C. took place and a new battalion of eleven companies was formed and located — Plymouth (headquarters and six companies), Devonport (3) and Tavistock (2). An increase in establishment to twelve companies was made in 1900, but a reduction to eight occurred during 1905.

3rd Volunteer Battalion. "SOUTH AFRICA 1901"

The original companies of the 3rd Volunteer Battalion at Exeter, previously the 3rd Devonshire R.V.C. and before that the County's 1st Administrative Battalion, were all raised during 1860/61 — Cullompton, Buckerell, Bampton, Honiton, Tiverton, Ottery St. Mary and Colyton. Additional companies were added, one each, at Sidmouth in 1885 and Axminster in 1900.

4th Volunteer Battalion. "SOUTH AFRICA 1900-01"

This battalion was formerlly Devonshire's 4th Corps and prior to that its 3rd Administrative Battalion. Dating from 1860, the

11. H.R.H. Prince Alfred of Edinburgh K.G., Lieutenant 2nd (Prince of Wales's) Volunteer Battalion, Devonshire Regiment, 1895.

Battalion had its headquarters at Barnstaple and at first comprised seven companies located — Barnstaple (2), Hatherleigh, Okehampton, Bideford, Torrington and South Molton. In 1896 an additional company was sanctioned, followed by two more in 1900 and another in 1901.

5th (The Hay Tor) Volunteer Battalion.
"SOUTH AFRICA 1900-01"
In 1880 the 4th Administrative Battalion of Devonshire Rifle Volunteers was consolidated as the County's 5th Corps at Newton Abbot, its six companies dating from 1860 and located at Ashburton, Newton Abbot, Totnes, Chudleigh, Kingsbridge and Torquay. In 1886 an additional two companies, one each at Buckfastleigh and Torquay, were sanctioned.

Uniform
The uniform and facing colours of the five battalions were — green/black (1st), green/scarlet (2nd), grey/green (3rd), scarlet/white (4th) and scarlet/green changing to scarlet/white in 1895 (5th).

Territorial Force
In 1908 the 1st and 3rd Volunteer Battalions were merged to form the 4th Battalion (TF) while the 2nd and 5th joined as 5th. At the same time the 4th Volunteer Battalion provided the Regiment's 6th Battalion.

SUFFOLK REGIMENT

The Counties of Suffolk and Cambridgeshire provided the battalions for the Suffolk Regiment. Previously Number 32 Sub-District Brigade, the Regiment was organised — 1st and 2nd Battalions (late 12th Foot), 3rd Battalion (late West Suffolk Militia), 4th Battalion (late Cambridge Militia) and two corps of rifle volunteers from each county. The title of the Regiment was assumed by all volunteer battalions in 1887.

1st Volunteer Battalion. "SOUTH AFRICA 1900-02"
When the 2nd Administrative Battalion of Suffolk Rifle Volunteers was consolidated as 1st Corps in 1880 its organisation was — Ipswich (3), Framlingham, Woodbridge, Halesworth, Saxmundham and Leiston. Headquarters were at first in Ipswich, changing to Woodbridge before the end of 1881, and then back to Ipswich in 1890. In 1900 the Framlingham Company ("D") was merged into "G" at Saxmundham, its place being taken by a new "D" Company in Ipswich. Also in 1900, and at Ipswich, a cyclist company was formed.

2nd Volunteer Battalion. "SOUTH AFRICA 1900-02"

The opportunity to take on the position of 2nd Corps was declined by the 1st Administrative Battalion upon consolidation in 1880. Instead it chose to retain the number held by its senior corps — 6th, and in doing so made Suffolk the only county without a clear run of numbers after 1880. Headquarters moved from Sudbury to Bury St. Edmunds in 1889 and the original eight companies were located at Stowmarket, Eye (2), Sudbury, Bury St Edmunds (2), Hadleigh and Newmarket.

3rd (Cambridgeshire) Volunteer Battalion. "SOUTH AFRICA 1900-01"

In 1880 the 1st Administrative Battalion of Cambridgeshire Rifle Volunteers was consolidated as the County's 1st Corps. With headquarters in Cambridge and ten companies, including one each in Essex and Hunts, the Battalion was located at Cambridge (4), Wisbech, Whittlesea, March, Ely, Saffron Walden and St. Neots. The Hunts company at St. Neots was disbanded in 1889.

Cambridge University Volunteer Rifle Corps. "SOUTH AFRICA 1900-01"

The services of a corps of rifle volunteers at the University were accepted by the War Office in December, 1859. Six companies were later formed from within the several colleges, and the title assumed was — 3rd Cambridgeshire Rifle Volunteer Corps. In 1880 the number of the Corps was changed to 2nd, the title — 4th (Cambridge University) Volunteer Battalion, Suffolk Regiment being adopted in 1887. In 1903, however, Army Order 56 of April announced that His Majesty the King has been graciously pleased to approve the new title — The Cambridge University Volunteer Rifle Corps. Two additional companies were sanctioned in 1900 and this remained the establishment up till 1908.

Uniform

In the Suffolk battalions green uniforms with black facings were worn by the 1st and grey with scarlet by the 2nd. The Cambridgeshires had scarlet with blue while at the University light blue facings were added to grey uniforms in 1892.

Territorial Force

The 4th and 5th Battalions (TF) were formed by the 1st and 2nd Volunteer Battalions respectively in 1908. At first the 3rd V.B. was titled as The Cambridgeshire Battalion of the Suffolk Regiment, but by 1909 this had been changed to The Cambridgeshire Regiment. The University became part of the Senior Division, Officers Training Corps.

29

12. Sergeant Instructor of Musketry, 2nd Volunteer Battalion, Suffolk Regiment.

PRINCE ALBERT'S
(SOMERSETSHIRE LIGHT INFANTRY)

In 1873 Number 36 Sub-District was formed out of the line, militia and volunteer battalions of the County of Somersetshire. This large county maintained seven infantry battalions and in 1881 these were organised into the Prince Albert's Light Infantry (Somersetshire Regiment)(the title changed before the end of the year) as follows:- 1st and 2nd Battalions (late 13th Foot), 3rd Battalion (late 1st Somersetshire Militia), 4th Battalion (late 2nd Somersetshire Militia) and three battalions of volunteers.

1st Volunteer Battalion. "SOUTH AFRICA 1900-01"
The senior volunteer battalion of the Somersetshire Light Infantry originated in 1860 when seven of the County's rifle companies, raised during 1859/60, were organised into the 1st Administrative Battalion of Somersetshire Rifle Volunteers. In 1880 this formation was consolidated as 1st Corps, and then in 1882, it assumed the title — 1st Volunteer Battalion. This was the first volunteer corps in the United Kingdom to take on the title of its regiment.

Headquarters of the Battalion were at Bath, its original seven companies being located at — Bath, Bathwick, Keynsham, Warleigh Manor, Lyncombe, Walcot and Kilmersdon. In 1885 an additional company was added and then in 1900 two others were raised bringing the Battalion's establishment up to ten companies.

2nd Volunteer Battalion. "SOUTH AFRICA 1900-01"
The origins of the 2nd Volunteer Battalion were similar to those of the 1st, the County's 2nd Administrative Battalion being formed in 1860 and comprising a number of Somerset corps. When the Volunteer Force was reorganised in 1880 the new consolidated battalion at first took on the number of its senior corps — the 3rd at Taunton. However, before the end of the year the title of 2nd Somersetshire Rifle Volunteer Corps had been assumed and then in 1882 this was changed to 2nd Volunteer Battalion.

With headquarters at Taunton the 2nd Volunteer Battalion maintained twelve companies — Taunton (2), Wellington, Williton, Wiveliscombe, Yeovil, Crewkerne, Langport, Bridgewater (3) and South Petherton. An increase to the establishment by one company was made in 1901.

3rd Volunteer Battalion. "SOUTH AFRICA 1900-01"
With headquarters at Wells, the 3rd Administrative Battalion of Somerset Rifle Volunteers was also formed in 1860. Upon

31

13. 2nd Volunteer Battalion, The Prince Albert's (Somersetshire Light Infantry). (J. Allen)

consolidation in 1880 nine independent corps were formed into one. Initially, the number of the senior corps (4th) was assumed, however, this was changed to 3rd before the end of 1880, and then in 1882 3rd Volunteer Battalion became the title.

Headquarters moved from Wells to Weston-Super-Mare in 1882 and the Battalion's original ten companies were located — Burnham, Weston-Super-Mare, Wells, Frome, Shepton Mallett, Glastonbury, Castle Cary, Keinton and Langford. Two companies were lost by the end of 1882, but the establishment was raised to nine during the Boer War.

Uniform
Various shades of grey uniforms were worn by the Somersetshire rifle volunteers. In 1877 the 1st Corps adopted scarlet with black facings and wore this until 1884 when Royal blue collars and cuffs were assumed. Both the 2nd and 3rd Battalions had grey uniforms with black facings.

Territorial Force
In 1908 the 1st, 2nd and 3rd Volunteer Battalions were merged to form the Regiment's two Territorial Battalions — 4th and 5th.

PRINCE OF WALES'S OWN (WEST YORKSHIRE REGIMENT)

The organisation of the senior Yorkshire regiment by the end of 1881 was — 1st and 2nd Battalions (late 14th Foot), 3rd Battalion (late 2nd Wek York Militia), 4th Battalion (late 4th West York Militia) and the 1st, 3rd and 7th Yorkshire West Riding Rifle Volunteer Corps. The three volunteer battalions assumed the title of the Regiment in 1887.

9th Yorkshire (West Riding) Rifle Volunteer Corps
The 9th, along with the 3rd and 7th Corps, were prior to 1881 part of Number 10 Sub-District Brigade. For a few months of 1881 the 9th Corps formed part of the West Yorkshire Regiment. By the end of the year, however, it had been transferred to the Duke of Wellington's Regiment and replaced by the 1st Corps.

1st Volunteer Battalion."SOUTH AFRICA 1900"
With headquarters in York, the Battalion had originated in 1859, served as the 1st Administrative Battalion of Yorkshire (West Riding) Rifle Volunteers and from 1880, the County's 1st Corps. In 1880 the strength of the 1st Corps stood at eleven

companies — York (5), Harrogate, Knaresborough, Ripon (2), Tadcaster and Selby. An additional company was sanctioned in 1900 and after the re-location of 'K' Company from Tadcaster to Pateley Bridge, the Battalion, in 1908, was situated — York (5), Harrogate (2), Knaresborough, Ripon (2), Pateley Bridge and Selby.

2nd Volunteer Battalion."SOUTH AFRICA 1900"
In 1860 a number of rifle volunteer companies formed in the previous year at Bradford were merged under the title of 5th Yorkshire (West Riding) Corps. This number was, in the same year, changed to 3rd. By 1880 the establishment of the Battalion stood at eight companies, a ninth comprising cyclists, being added in 1900.

3rd Volunteer Battalion."SOUTH AFRICA 1900"
The Regiment's 3rd Volunteer Battalion was the "Leeds Rifles" and had been formed in the City at the end of 1859. Originally numbered as 11th Corps, this changed to 7th in 1860, the strength of the Battalion was ten companies.

Uniform
Both the 1st and 2nd Volunteer Battalions wore scarlet, the 1st changing from blue facings to white and the 2nd, dark green to white around 1888. Both battalions are then shown in the Army List, from 1904, as having adopted the buff facings of the line battalions. The 3rd Volunteer Battalion wore green with black facings.

Territorial Force
The Regiment's 5th and 6th Battalions were formed in order of seniority by the 1st and 2nd Volunteer Battalions. The 3rd provided a 'double battalion' numbered 7th and 8th.

14. Pouch belt plate, 3rd Volunteer Battalion, West Yorkshire Regiment.

EAST YORKSHIRE REGIMENT

Prior to 1881 the East Riding of Yorkshire provided the several battalions comprising Number 5 Sub-District Brigade. The East Yorkshire Regiment was formed from these and in 1881 comprised — 1st and 2nd Battalions (late 15th Foot), 3rd Battalion (late East Yorks Militia) and the 1st and 2nd Yorkshire East Riding Rifle Volunteer Corps. The volunteers assumed the title of the Regiment in 1883.

1st Volunteer Battalion."SOUTH AFRICA 1900-01"
In 1861 the several rifle volunteer corps that had been formed in Hull during 1859/60 were merged into one corps designated as 1st Yorkshire (East Riding). Additional personnel were sanctioned in 1896 increasing the original establishment of six companies to eight.

2nd Volunteer Battalion."SOUTH AFRICA 1900-01"
Upon consolidation of the 1st Administrative Battalion of Yorkshire (East Riding) Rifle Volunteers in 1880, the number at first assumed was that of its senior corps, the 3rd (formed 1860). This was changed to 2nd, however, within a few months.

With headquarters in Beverley, the Battalion's original six companies were located at Howden, Bridlington, Beverley, Driffield, Market Weighton and Pocklington.

15. Maxim Gun detachment, 1st Volunteer Battalion, East Yorkshire Regiment.

Uniform

Until 1882 the uniforms shown in the Army List are for 1st Corps, scarlet with yellow facings, and for 2nd, scarlet with buff. In that year both battalions are listed as having white facings.

Territorial Force

In 1908 the 1st Volunteer Battalion became the Regiment's 4th Battalion (TF). At the same time the 2nd Volunteer Battalion provided four companies of the 5th Battalion Yorkshire Regiment (TF).

16. Cap badge, 1st (Hertfordshire) Volunteer Battalion, Bedfordshire Regiment. (Lt. Col. J.D. Sainsbury TD).

BEDFORDSHIRE REGIMENT

The Regiment was formed out of Number 33 Sub-District, less the Huntingdonshire Militia which became 5th Battalion, King's Royal Rifle Corps. Line battalions (1st and 2nd) were formerlly the 16th Foot, and the militia (3rd and 4th Battalions) that of the Counties of Bedfordshire and Hertfordshire respectively. These same counties also supplied the volunteers of the Regiment, Hertfordshire providing two corps while Bedfordshire contributed one. Under General Order 181 of 1887 the two units of the former county were redesignated as — 1st (Hertfordshire) and 2nd (Hertfordshire) Volunteer Battalions. At the same time the 1st Bedfordshire Rifle Volunteer Corps became the 3rd Volunteer Battalion. Later, in 1900, a fourth battalion of volunteers was formed in the County of Huntingdonshire and added to the Regiment.

1st (Hertfordshire) Volunteer Battalion.
"SOUTH AFRICA 1900-02"

The 2nd Administrative Battalion of Hertfordshire Rifle Volunteers was formed with headquarters at Hertford in 1860. Containing five Hertfordshire Corps raised between 1859-1876, and one from Essex, the Battalion was consolidated in 1880 as the 1st Hertfordshire Rifle Volunteer Corps. At first eight companies were located at Hertford (2), Bishop's Stortford, Ware, Royston, Welwyn, Hitchin and Waltham Abbey. In 1900 the establishment of the Battalion was increased to nine companies when new personnel were recruited at Hoddesdon.

2nd (Hertfordshire) Volunteer Battalion.
"SOUTH AFRICA 1900-02"

In 1881 the five companies of the 2nd Hertfordshire Rifle Volunteer Corps, formerlly the County's 1st Administrative Battalion and dating from 1860, were located at Watford, St. Albans, Ashridge, Hemel Hempstead and Berkhampstead. Later, new companies were formed at Tring in 1883, Watford in 1892 and Apsley in 1900. The latter was disbanded in 1904 and Battalion Headquarters moved from Little Gaddesden to Hemel Hempstead in 1901.

3rd Volunteer Battalion. "SOUTH AFRICA 1900-02"

The origins of the 1st Bedfordshire Rifle Volunteer Corps, Headquarters at Bedford, lay in the eight rifle corps formed in the County between 1860-1864. These provided the original nine company strength of the 3rd Volunteer Battalion and were located at Bedford (2), Toddington, Dunstable, Ampthill, Luton (2), Shefford and Woburn.

4th (Hunts) Volunteer Battalion

The County of Huntingdonshire was without infantry volunteers from 1889 until late 1900 when the 4th (Hunts) Volunteer Battalion, headquarters Huntingdon, was raised and added to the Bedfordshire Regiment. Mainly recruited around the Huntingdon, St. Ives, Fletton and St. Neots areas, the Battalion consisted of eight, later six, companies.

Uniform

Both the 1st and 3rd Volunteer Battalions adopted the uniform of the Bedfordshire Regiment (scarlet with white facings) — the 1st in 1897 and the 3rd by 1885. Previously, the 1st had worn grey and scarlet while the 3rd had scarlet and yellow. The 2nd retained its grey right up to 1908, green facings being exchanged for grey in 1887. The 4th wore drab.

Territorial Force
In 1908 most of the 1st and 2nd Volunteer Battalions formed a single battalion, later to be known as the Hertfordshire Regiment. Both the 3rd and 4th Volunteer Battalions remained with the Bedfordshire Regiment providing four companies each of its 5th Battalion (TF).

LEICESTERSHIRE REGIMENT

The Rifle Volunteers of Leicestershire first became associated with the 17th Regiment of Foot (later 1st and 2nd Leicestershire Regiment) in 1873 when together with the 45th Foot, the Leicestershire Militia and the Militia and Volunteers of Nottinghamshire it comprised Number 27 Sub-District.

In 1881 Regimental District Number 17 was formed out of the Leicestershire elements of Number 27 Sub-District. This, the Leicestershire Regiment, comprised the 1st and 2nd Battalions (17th Foot), the Leicestershire Militia which formed the 3rd and later 4th Battalions of the Regiment and the 1st Leicestershire Rifle Volunteer Corps. The latter was subsequently redesignated in 1883 (General Order 14) as the 1st Volunteer Battalion, Leicestershire Regiment.

1st Volunteer Battalion. "SOUTH AFRICA 1900-02"
This, the only volunteer component of the Regiment, originated in 1859 upon the formation at Leicester of the 1st Leicestershire Rifle Volunteer Corps. The County later raised nine other independent units which were subsequently organised into a battalion and later a single corps.

In 1881 headquarters of the Battalion were in Leicester, its strength being eleven companies located as follows:- Leicester (6), Belvoir, Melton Mowbray, Loughborough, Ashby-de-la-Zouch, and Hinckley. In the following year a new company was formed at Market Harborough and in 1900 the establishment was again increased when four more companies — Leicester (2), Wigston, Mountsorrel were sanctioned.

Uniform
The 1st Leicestershire Rifle Volunteers had worn scarlet for many years, yellow facings being exchanged for white in 1879.

17. Fifes and Drums, 1st Volunteer Battalion, Leicestershire Regiment. (John Woodroff).

Territorial Force
With its sixteen companies the Battalion was, in 1908, called upon to furnish the two Territorial battalions that had been allotted to the Leicestershire Regiment under the new system. This was carried out by merging the Leicester and Wigston Companies as 4th Battalion while the 5th was formed by the remainder less the Belvoir Company which was disbanded.

ALEXANDRA, PRINCESS OF WALES'S OWN (YORKSHIRE REGIMENT)

The Princess of Wales's Own (Yorkshire Regiment) (title changed to the above in 1902) was created in 1881 out of the battalions then comprising Number 4 Sub-District together with the 5th West Yorkshire Militia — 1st and 2nd Battalions (late 19th Foot), 3rd Battalion (late 5th West Yorks Militia), 4th Battalion (late North Yorks Militia) and the 1st and 2nd Yorkshire North Riding Rifle Volunteer Corps. Redesignation as Volunteer Battalions took place in 1883.

1st Volunteer Battalion. "SOUTH AFRICA 1900-02"
The senior company of the 1st Volunteer Battalion was formed in 1860 as the 4th Yorkshire (North Riding) Rifle Volunteer Corps, and together with other North Riding Corps formed the County's 1st Administrative Battalion. When the Battalion was consolidated in 1880 the number at first assumed was that of the 4th Corps. This, however, was changed to 1st within a few months.

Headquarters were in Richmond (moving to Northallerton in 1883) and the Battalion's original nine company establishment located at — Thornton Rust, Bedale, Stokesley, Catterick, Richmond, Reeth, Skelton, Northallerton and Guisborough. After a number of relocations, amalgamations, disbandments, and in 1884 the formation of a new company, by 1893 locations were — Leyburn, Bedale, Stokesley, Catterick, Richmond, Skelton, Northallerton, Thirsk, Guisborough and Wensleydale. After further changes company locations in 1898 were — Middleham, Bedale, Stokesley, Catterick, Richmond, Redcar, Skelton, Northallerton, Thirsk and Guisborough, and then by 1908 — Bedale, Eston, Stokesley, Catterick, Richmond, Redcar, Skelton, Northallerton, Thirsk and Guisborough.

2nd Volunteer Battalion. "SOUTH AFRICA 1900-02"
The 2nd Volunteer Battalion was formerlly the 2nd Yorkshire (North Riding) Rifle Volunteer Corps and before that the County's 2nd Administrative Battalion. With headquarters in

18. Group of officers, including Sir William Cayley Worsley, Bt. (Commanding Officer), 2nd Yorkshire (North Riding) Rifle Volunteer Corps, 1881. (Green Howards Regimental Museum)

Scarborough the Battalion comprised seven companies, their original locations being — Malton, Hovingham (2), Scarborough (2), Helmsley, and Pickering.

Uniform
The scarlet jackets of the 1st Volunteer Battalion at first had green facings, the Army List in 1885 indicating that by this time a change had been made to white. Grey uniforms with scarlet facings were originally worn by the 2nd Volunteer Battalion, but this was soon changed to scarlet with green facings.

Territorial Force
In 1908 the 1st Volunteer Battalion became the Regiment's 4th Battalion (TF) while the 2nd formed part of the 5th.

LANCASHIRE FUSILIERS

Number 17 Sub-District Brigade provided the several battalions of the Lancashire Fusiliers in 1881 — 1st and 2nd (late 20th Foot), 3rd (late 7th Royal Lancashire Militia) and the 8th and 12th Lancashire Rifle Volunteer Corps. The two volunteer battalions assumed the title of the Regiment in 1883 and in 1886 the 17th Lancashire RVC was transferred from the Manchester Regiment and assumed the title of 3rd Volunteer Battalion.

1st Volunteer Battalion. "SOUTH AFRICA 1900-02"
The 8th Lancashire Rifle Volunteer Corps was formed with headquarters at Bury in 1859. Six companies were maintained — Bury (4), Heywood (2) until 1883 when sanction to form an additional two at Bury was received.

2nd Volunteer Battalion. "SOUTH AFRICA 1900-02"
Formed as the 24th Lancashire Rifle Volunteer Corps at Rochdale in 1860 and re-numbered as 12th in 1880. The Battalion maintained a strength of seven companies, at least one being located outside Rochdale at Middleton.

3rd Volunteer Battalion. "SOUTH AFRICA 1900-02"
This battalion was formed as the 56th Lancashire Rifle Volunteer Corps at Salford in 1860. It became 17th in 1880 and prior to joining the Lancashire Fusiliers as 3rd VB in 1886 served as a volunteer battalion of the Manchester Regiment. The strength of the Battalion was increased from eight

19. Officer and senior NCOs, 1st Volunteer Battalion, Lancashire Fusiliers. Conway camp 1890. (Lancashire Fusiliers Regimental Museum)

companies to ten in 1897 and then to sixteen in 1900. The 3rd Volunteer Battalion, Lancashire Fusiliers was one of the largest battalions, returning some 1,710 all ranks in 1907.

Uniform
All three battalions were wearing scarlet uniforms with white facings by 1886; the 1st previously having yellow facings while the 2nd and 3rd had blue.

Territorial Force
In 1908 the 1st VB provided the Regiment's 5th Battalion (TF), the 2nd VB its 6th and the 3rd VB a double battalion — 7th and 8th.

ROYAL SCOTS FUSILIERS

When formed in 1881, the Regiment comprised the several battalions formerlly of Number 61 Sub-District Brigade — 1st and 2nd Battalion (late 21st Foot), 3rd Battalion (late Scottish Borderers Militia) and 4th Battalion (late Royal Ayr and Wigtown Militia). The original volunteers were those corps from Ayrshire, Dumfrieshire, Galloway and Roxburgh & Selkirk.

1st Volunteer Battalion. "SOUTH AFRICA 1900-02"
Redesignated in 1887, the Battalion was formerlly the 1st Ayrshire Rifle Volunteer Corps and prior to 1880, the County's 2nd Administrative Battalion. With headquarters in Kilmarnock the Battalion's original establishment of eight companies were located at Kilmarnock, Irvine, Largs, Beith, Saltcoats, Dalry, Darvel and Galston.

In 1900 a number of changes in organisation took place. Two new companies, one a cyclist, were formed at Kilmarnock, and during the same year the Largs Company ("C") moved to Stewarton, while the headquarters of "H" were transferred from Galston to Kilmarnock.

2nd Volunteer Battalion. "SOUTH AFRICA 1900-01"
In 1880 the 2nd Ayrshire Rifle Volunteer Corps, previously the 1st Adminstrative Battalion, comprised headquarters at Ayr and seven companies located — Ayr (2), Maybole, Girvan, Cumnock, Sorn and Newmilns. A new company, at Troon, was formed in 1883 and in the same year the headquarters of the Sorn Company were moved to Catrine. Redesignation as 2nd Volunteer Battalion was in 1887 and in 1900 a cyclist company was raised at Ayr.

20. Colour-Sergeant Galloway, 2nd Volunteer Battalion, Royal Scots Fusiliers. Ex Champion Shot of Scotland.

45

1st Dumfrieshire Rifle Volunteer Corps
This corps served as a volunteer battalion of the Regiment until 1887 when it was transferred to the King's Own Scottish Borderers.

The Galloway Rifle Volunteer Corps
Part of the Regiment until transfer to the King's Own Scottish Borderers in 1899.

1st Roxburgh and Selkirk (The Border) Rifle Volunteer Corps
Part of the Regiment until transfer to the King's Own Scottish Borderers in 1887.

Uniform
Both battalions wore scarlet tunics with blue facings. In 1888, the 1st changed to the doublets and Black Watch pattern tartan trews of the Regiment, as did the 2nd in 1898.

Territorial Force
The 4th and 5th Battalions (TF) were formed by the 1st and 2nd Volunteer Battalions in 1908.

21. White metal pouch belt plate, 1st Cheshire Rifle Volunteer Corps. (Badge provided for photography by Steven Bosley)

CHESHIRE REGIMENT

The Cheshire Regiment was formed out of Number 18 Sub-District which in 1881 comprised the 22nd Regiment of Foot (1st and 2nd Bns), 1st Royal Cheshire Militia (3rd Bn), 2nd Royal Cheshire Militia (4th Bn) and the 1st to 5th Cheshire Rifle Volunteer Corps. The volunteers assumed the title of the Regiment in 1887.

1st Volunteer Battalion. "SOUTH AFRICA 1900-02"

The first company of Cheshire rifle volunteers was raised at Birkenhead in 1859. The following year, this and other corps were grouped as the County's 1st Administrative Battalion, which subsequently, in 1880, was consolidated to form the 1st Cheshire Rifle Volunteer Corps. With headquarters in Birkenhead, the 1st Corps originally comprised eight companies — Birkenhead, Oxton, Egremont, New Ferry, Neston, Hooton, Tranmere and Bromborough.

With the increase in volunteers brought about by the war in South Africa, an additional four companies were sanctioned for the Battalion in 1900. Now consisting of twelve companies, the Battalion, in 1901, is recorded as — Birkenhead six companies, Tranmere two, Liscard two and Neston two. By 1907, however, one of the Neston Companies appears to have moved to Heswall.

2nd (Earl of Chester's) Volunteer Battalion. "SOUTH AFRICA 1900-02"

The County's 2nd Administrative Battalion was also formed in 1860 and included among its corps the 6th Cheshire. Raised in 1859, the 6th was granted the additional title "Earl of Chester's" in 1870. In 1880 the 2nd Admin. was consolidated as 2nd Corps, the "Earl of Chester's" title being carried on by the new corps, and later as 2nd Volunteer Battalion.

Headquarters of the Battalion were at Chester where five of its original nine companies were also located. Others were at Runcorn (2), Weaverham and Frodsham. the Battalion's establishment was increased to eleven companies in 1900 — these, by 1908, being located — Chester (6½), Hartford (2), Runcorn and Frodsham (1½). In its last return, the 2nd (Earl of Chester's) Volunteer Battalion recorded 1,081 all ranks.

3rd Volunteer Battalion. "SOUTH AFRICA 1900-02"

The senior company of the 3rd Volunteer Battalion was formed in 1860 and that year joined with other Cheshire corps, the County's 3rd Administrative Battalion. In 1880 the 3rd Admin. became the 3rd Corps, its headquarters being at Knutsford and with a strength of eight companies. This establishment was maintained until 1908, companies being located at

47

Altrincham (2), Knutsford, Northwich, Winsford, Cheadle, Sale and Lymm. In its 1907 return, the Battalion recorded 736 enrolled volunteers.

4th Volunteer Battalion. "SOUTH AFRICA 1900-02"
In addition to Cheshire corps, the 4th Administrative Battalion of Cheshire Rifle Volunteers also included from Glossop, the 23rd Derbyshire Corps. Formed in 1860, the Battalion was consolidated as 4th Corps in 1880. Its headquarters were placed at Stockport and an establishment of thirteen companies was maintained originally at Stalybridge (3), Stockport (6), Hyde and Glossop (3). Some 1,066 enrolled volunteers were returned in 1907.

5th Volunteer Battalion.
The 5th Volunteer Battalion was formerlly the 5th Cheshire Rifle Volunteer Corps, and before that the County's 5th Administrative Battalion. With headquarters at Congleton, the Battalion maintained ten companies, their original locations being — Congleton (2), Macclesfield (4), Sandbach, Wilmslow (2) and Nantwich. The Battalion's last return recorded a strength of 836 all ranks out of an establishment of 1,160 and is one of the few that carries no South African war honour.

Uniform
Two battalions, the 1st and 5th, wore grey uniforms with scarlet facings. Scarlet with buff facings are recorded for the 2nd, while the 3rd and 4th are shown with scarlet and white. The latter, according to the Army List, changing from buff facings in 1889.

Territorial Force
Upon transfer to the Territorial Force in 1908 the 1st, 4th and 5th Volunteer Battalions became the Regiment's 4th, 6th and 7th Battalions respectively. With only four infantry battalions allotted to the Cheshire area an amalgamation between the 2nd and 3rd Volunteer Battalions took place. The merger provided the 5th (Earl of Chester's) Battalion.

ROYAL WELSH FUSILIERS

In 1881 No 23 Sub-District Brigade comprised the 23rd Regiment of Foot together with the militia and volunteer forces of the Counties of Carnarvonshire, Denbighshire, Flintshire and Merionethshire. Consequently, upon the formation of the Royal Welsh Fusiliers, the 23rd became the 1st and 2nd

Battalions, while the Militia of Denbigh, Merioneth and Carnarvon became the Regiment's 3rd and 4th Battalions. At the same time, two corps — the 1st Denbigh and 1st Flint & Carnarvon, provided the volunteers, and these were re-designated as Volunteer Battalions in 1884.

22. Officers pouch belt plate, 2nd Volunteer Battalion, Royal Welsh Fusiliers.

1st Volunteer Battalion. "SOUTH AFRICA 1900-02"

Denbighshire provided the 1st Volunteer Battalion of the Royal Welsh Fusiliers, its earliest company being formed at Wrexham in 1859. The County's 1st Administrative Battalion was formed in 1860. It included all nine numbered corps that were raised, and in 1880 was consolidated as the 1st Denbighshire Rifle Volunteer Corps.

At the time of consolidation the 1st Corps comprised eight companies — Wrexham (2), Ruabon, Denbigh, Gresford, Gwersyllt, Ruthin and Llangollen. Headquarters were at Ruabon, but in 1881 this was moved to Wynnstay, and then four years later, to Wrexham. When the Battalion transferred to the Territorial Force in 1908 its strength stood at eleven companies, an additional three having been raised during 1900.

2nd Volunteer Battalion. "SOUTH AFRICA 1900-02"

All six numbered rifle corps that were raised in Flintshire between 1860-1872 were included in the county's 1st Administrative Battalion. In 1873 the administrative battalion in the neighbouring county of Carnarvonshire was broken up and its five corps subsequently transferred to Flintshire. When the Volunteer Force was reorganised in 1880 the several rifle corps then existing within the two Counties were merged, the new corps of ten companies being styled — 1st Flintshire & Carnarvonshire.

The original companies of the new battalion were provided; six in Flintshire — Mold, Hawarden, Rhyl, Holywell, Flint, Caergwle; and four in Carnarvonshire — Carnarvon (2), Portmadoc, Llanberis. By 1897 over half of the Battalion's strength, now sixteen companies, was provided by Carnarvonshire and subsequently it was decided to form a separate battalion out of the County's volunteers. Consequently the 2nd Volunteer Battalion was reduced to an establishment of eight companies.

In 1897 Battalion Headquarters were moved from Rhyl to Hawarden. Three years later an additional three companies were sanctioned then, in 1904 a reduction was made to ten. At the time of transfer to the Territorial Force in 1908 the strength of the Battalion stood at 958 all ranks out of an establishment of 1,164.

3rd Volunteer Battalion. "SOUTH AFRICA 1900-02"

As mentioned above, the eight Carnarvonshire companies of the 2nd Volunteer Battalion were made independent in 1897. Headquarters were placed at Carnarvon and in 1900 Anglesey, without rifle volunteers since the disbandment of its last corps in 1863, provided a new company at Holyhead. In the last year of the Volunteer system the strength of the 3rd Volunteer

Battalion stood at 836 all ranks; its nine companies being distributed at Carnarvon (2), Portmadoc, Penygroes, Llanberis, Conway, Penmaenmawr, Pwllheli and Holyhead.

Uniform
All three volunteer battalions wore the uniform of the Royal Welsh Fusiliers — scarlet with blue facings. The 2nd Volunteer Battalion, however, began with green facings, the change to blue not being indicated in the Army List until 1888.

Territorial Force
In 1908 the three volunteer battalions of the Royal Welsh Fusiliers provided, respectively, the Regiment's 4th, 5th and 6th Battalions (TF).

23. Lieut-Col. Edward Pryce-Jones, Commanding Officer 5th Volunteer Battalion, South Wales Borderers.

SOUTH WALES BORDERERS

The regiments previously comprising Number 25 Sub-District, together with the Royal Montgomery Militia, formed the South Wales Borderers in 1881 — 1st and 2nd Battalions (late 24th Foot), 3rd Battalion (late Royal South Wales Borderers Militia) and 4th Battalion (late Royal Montgomery Militia). The volunteers were from Brecknockshire and Monmouthshire and these assumed the title of the Regiment in 1885.

1st (Brecknockshire) Volunteer Battalion. "SOUTH AFRICA 1900-01"

The County of Brecknockshire had only one rifle volunteer corps from 1880. This was previously the 1st Administrative Battalion and comprised companies formed between 1859-1878. With headquarters in Brecon, the Battalion's original eight companies were located at Brecon (2), Brynmawr, Crickhowell, Hay, Builth, Talgarth and Cefn. A new company was formed at Ystradgynlais in 1894.

2nd Volunteer Battalion. "SOUTH AFRICA 1900-02"

The 1st Administrative Battalion of Monmouthshire Rifle Volunteers was formed in 1860 and in 1880 became the 1st Monmouthshire Rifle Volunteer Corps. With headquarters in Newport, the Battalion's original seven companies were located at Chepstow, Newport (2), Pontymister (2), Tredegar and Bassaleg. Additional personnel were added in 1882, 1892 and during the Boer War, and by 1905 a strength of ten companies was located — Chepstow, Newport (4), Tredegar, Pontymister, Blackwood, Rogerstone and Rhymney.

3rd Volunteer Battalion. "SOUTH AFRICA 1900-02"

Pontypool was the headquarters of the 3rd Volunteer Battalion, the 2nd Monmouthshire Rifle Volunteer corps being formed there in 1859. By 1881 the establishment of the Battalion stood at seven companies, their headquarters being at Pontypool, Ebbw Vale (2), Abersychan, Sirhowy, Panteg and Garndiffaith. In 1884 a new company was raised at Victoria but in 1897 this was moved to Abertillery. Also, by this time, the Panteg company had moved to Upper Pontnewydd and in the following year one of the Ebbw Vale companies transferred to Newbridge. With the increase in volunteers during the war in South Africa, two new companies were formed — "I" at Abercarn in 1900 and "K" (Cyclist) at Ebbw Vale in the following year. The year 1900 also saw the headquarters of "C" (Upper Pontnewydd) Company moved to Cwmbran. The cyclists were disbanded in 1903 which was to leave the Battalion with an establishment of nine companies —

Pontypool, Garndiffaith, Cwmbran, Ebbw Vale, Newbridge, Sirhowy, Abersychan (Pontypool by 1905), Abertillery and Abercarn, through to 1908.

4th Volunteer Battalion. "SOUTH AFRICA 1900-02"
This battalion dates from 1860 and the formation at Pontypool of the 2nd Administrative Battalion of Monmouthshire Rifle Volunteers. The 2nd was consolidated as 3rd Corps in 1880 and at that time comprised eight companies located — Blaenavon, Pontypool, Monmouth, Newport (3), Usk and Abergavenny. Later additions to the Battalion in 1895 and 1900, increased its establishment to ten companies, these in 1905 being located at — Blaenavon, Pontypool, Newport (4), Usk, Abergavenny (2) and Monmouth. Battalion Headquarters moved from Pontypool to Newport in 1901.

5th Volunteer Battalion. "SOUTH AFRICA 1900-01"
The 5th Volunteer Battalion was formed with headquarters at Newtown, Montgomeryshire in 1897. At first the formation of four companies was sanctioned but within a few months permission to increase the establishment to six had been received. From 1898 to 1901 the headquarters of the Battalion's six companies were located at — Newtown (2), Welshpool, Machynlleth, Aberdovey and Towyn. In 1901 "E" (Aberdovey) Company moved to Aberystwith University College.

Uniform
Referring to the Army List for information on colours worn; the 2nd Volunteer Battalion is shown as having retained its green uniforms and black facings through to 1908. The 1st, 3rd, 4th and 5th are all shown as wearing scarlet with white facings up till 1908: the 1st changing from grey with black facings in 1884, the 3rd exchanging grass green facings for the white in 1885, the 4th, also green and black, adopting the scarlet in 1887 and the 5th with scarlet and white from its formation.

According to "The Historical Records of the Yeomanry and Volunteers of Montgomeryshire" by Lieut-Col. R.W. Williams Wynn, DSO, the 5th Volunteer Battalion received permission to adopt the grass green facings of the South Wales Borderers in 1905.

It is also possible that the 4th had changed to grass green by 1908. A photograph taken just after transfer to the Territorial Force shows tunics with volunteer designation on the shoulder straps still being worn, but collars and cuffs are of a dark material.

Territorial Force
In 1908 the 1st Volunteer Battalion became known as The Brecknockshire Battalion, The South Wales Borderers. At the

same time the 2nd, 3rd and 4th provided the three battalions of the Monmouthshire Regiment and the 5th joined the Royal Welsh Fusiliers as part of its 7th Battalion (TF).

KING'S OWN SCOTTISH BORDERERS

Prior to 1881 the two battalions of the 25th Foot formed part of Number 6 Sub-District Brigade. That year the 25th formed the 1st and 2nd Battalions, King's Own Borderers, but at that time no militia or volunteer units were attached. It was not until 1887 that the Scottish Borderers Militia joined as 3rd Battalion, while at the same time three Scottish rifle corps became volunteer battalions. In the same year the Regiment also added the word "Scottish" to its title.

1st Roxburgh and Selkirk (The Border) Volunteer Rifle Corps. "SOUTH AFRICA 1900-02"
This corps joined the Regiment in 1887 from the Royal Scots Fusiliers, its origins laying in the rifle volunteer companies formed in the Counties of Roxburghshire and Selkirkshire during 1859/60. Although ranked as 1st Volunteer Battalion, the 1st Roxburgh and Selkirk did not assume the title of the Regiment. At the time of transfer battalion headquarters were at Newtown St. Boswells (moved to Melrose in 1903) and a nine company establishment was located at Jedburgh, Kelso, Melrose, Hawick (2), Galashiels (2) and Selkirk (2). Before the end of 1887, one of the Selkirk Companies had been moved to Galashiels.

In 1892 a new company was formed at Hawick, two more followed in 1901, but these were disbanded after two years. The last addition to the Battalion was in 1903 when the cyclists of each company were grouped together as "L" (Cyclist) Company at Newcastleton.

2nd (Berwickshire) Volunteer Battalion. "SOUTH AFRICA 1900-02"
Dating from 1859, the Battalion was previously with the Royal Scots and known as the 1st Berwickshire Rifle Volunteer Corps. At the time of transfer the Battalion comprised — headquarters at Duns and seven companies — Duns, Coldstream, Ayton, Greenlaw, Lauderdale, Earlston and Chirnside. In 1891 a new company ('H') was formed at Duns. Another, 'I' at Ladykirk, was raised in 1900, but five years later this was re-lettered as 'H' due to the disbandment of the new Duns Company.

24. 1st Roxburgh and Selkirk (The Border) Volunteer Rifle Corps. (King's Own Scottish Borderers Regimental Museum).

3rd (Dumfries) Volunteer Battalion.
"SOUTH AFRICA 1900-02"
There were nine independent rifle corps formed within the County of Dumfriesshire during 1860/61. In 1861 these were organised into an administrative battalion which in 1880 was consolidated as 1st Corps. Headquarters of the new 1st Dumfriesshire Rifle Volunteer Corps were placed at Dumfries, its ten company establishment being located at Dumfries (2), Thornhill, Sanquhar, Penpont, Annan, Moffat, Langholm, Lockerbie and Lochmaben. In 1885 the Penpoint Company ('E') was merged into that at Thornhill and in its place a new 'E' Company was raised at Ecclefechan.

Between 1881 and 1887 the Corps served as a volunteer battalion of the Royal Scots Fusiliers. The year after transfer the headquarters of 'K' company at Lochmaben were moved to Canonbie.

The Galloway Volunteer Rifle Corps.
"SOUTH AFRICA 1900-02"
Galloway is the district of South West Scotland comprising the Counties of Wigtown and Kirkcudbright. The Rifle Volunteer corps formed within those areas were in 1860 grouped together under the title of The Galloway Administrative Battalion and in 1880 consolidated as the Galloway Rifle Volunteer Corps.

The Galloway Rifles joined the Royal Scots Fusiliers as one of its volunteer battalions in 1881. In 1899 the Corps was transferred to the King's Own Scottish Borderers and without change in title assumed the position of 4th Volunteer Battalion.

Headquarters of the Battalion were originally at Newton Stewart, moving to Castle Douglas in 1885 and then to Maxwelltown in 1904. There were eight companies located — Kirkcudbright, Castle Douglas, Stranraer, Newton Stewart, New Galloway, Maxwelltown (2) and Dalbeattie.

Uniform
Both the Border and Galloway Rifles wore grey uniforms, the latter having scarlet facings. In the 2nd and 3rd Volunteer Battalions, scarlet with blue facings were worn, the 3rd changing from scarlet/yellow in 1888. Both the numbered volunteer battalions adopted, along with the Regiment, Leslie tartan trews in 1900.

Territorial Force
In 1908 the 1st Roxburgh and Selkirk V.R.C. together with the 2nd V.B. formed the Regiment's 4th Battalion (TF). At the same time the 3rd V.B. and Galloway Rifles provided the 5th.

CAMERONIANS (SCOTTISH RIFLES)

The Cameronians originally comprised two regular battalions (formerly 26th and 90th Foot), two militia battalions (formerly 2nd Royal Lanark Militia) and five volunteer battalions.

1st Lanarkshire Volunteer Rifle Corps.
"SOUTH AFRICA 1900-02"

The senior rifle corps in Lanarkshire was formed in 1859 and comprised sixteen companies from the Glasgow area. The Corps served as the Regiment's 1st Volunteer Battalion, but this title was never assumed.

25. Hon. Colonel John A. Roxburgh V.D. Lieut-Colonel Commandant, 1st Lanarkshire Volunteer Rifle Corps 1906-1908.

2nd Volunteer Battalion. "SOUTH AFRICA 1900-02"

In 1873 a number of Lanarkshire rifle corps, then forming the County's 1st Administrative Battalion, were amalgamated under the title of its senior company — 16th. When the Volunteer Force was reorganised in 1880 the 16th became the 2nd and in 1887 assumed the title of the regiment. Headquarters of the Battalion were in Hamilton and its original ten companies located at Hamilton (2), Uddingston, Strathaven, Bothwell, Wishaw (2), Blantyre and Motherwell (2).

The Strathaven company ('D') was re-lettered as 'K' after an amalgamation in 1892 with 'K' at Motherwell. At the same time a new company was raised at Larkhall and lettered as 'D'. The Battalion's Cyclist company was formed at Hamilton in 1899 and in 1904 the headquarters of 'K' was moved from Strathaven to Motherwell.

3rd Lanarkshire Volunteer Rifle Corps. "SOUTH AFRICA 1900-02"

The 3rd Lanarkshire Volunteers was formed in 1860 by the amalgamation in Glasgow of a number of the City's rifle corps. In 1881 the Corps provided the Regiment's 3rd Volunteer Battalion, however this title was never assumed. Originally comprising twelve companies, the Battalion added its cyclist company in 1902.

4th Volunteer Battalion. "SOUTH AFRICA 1900-02"

The original title of this battalion, formed in Glasgow in 1859, was 4th Lanarkshire (Glasgow, 1st Northern) Rifle Volunteer Corps. The establishment of the Battalion was nine companies and in 1887 it assumed the title of the regiment.

5th Volunteer Battalion.

The 4th Administrative Battalion of Lanarkshire Rifle Volunteers was formed at Airdrie in 1862 and in 1873 was consolidated under the title of 29th Lanarkshire Rifle Volunteer Corps. Redesignated as 7th Corps in 1880, and then as 5th Volunteer Battalion in 1887, the Battalion comprised eight companies — Coatbridge (2), Airdrie (2), Shotts, Cheyston, Caldecruix and Newarthill.

On 1 April 1897 the 5th Volunteer Battalion was disbanded as a result of severe criticism by the officer commanding 26th Regimental District regarding its discipline.

Uniform

Only the 1st Lanarkshire VRC did not adopt scarlet, retaining the Elcho grey and blue facings taken into use in 1860. Both the 2nd Volunteer Battalion and 3rd Lanarkshire had blue facings, while the 4th and 5th Volunteer Battalions wore green and yellow respectively.

Territorial Force
There were four Territorial Force battalions (5th-8th) formed in 1908, these being provided by the Regiment's four volunteer battalions in order of seniority.

GLOUCESTERSHIRE REGIMENT

Number 37 Sub-District Brigade comprised two line battalions — the 28th and 61st Foot, two militia battalions — the Royal South and Royal North Gloucester and two regiments of volunteers — the 1st and 2nd Gloucestershire Rifle Volunteer Corps. These units formed the Gloucestershire Regiment in 1881.

1st (City of Bristol) Volunteer Battalion.
"SOUTH AFRICA 1900-02"
This battalion was designated as the above in 1883, having been previously the 1st Gloucestershire (City of Bristol) Rifle Volunteer Corps. Formed in 1859 the Corps soon comprised ten companies, adding an eleventh in 1902.

2nd Volunteer Battalion. "SOUTH AFRICA 1900-02"
In 1880 the ten Gloucestershire rifle corps then included in the County's 1st Administrative Battalion were consolidated as the 2nd Gloucestershire Rifle Volunteer Corps. This corps, which was redesignated as 2nd Volunteer Battalion in 1883, had its headquarters at Gloucester and eleven companies located at Gloucester Dock, Gloucester, Stroud, Cirencester, Cheltenham (2), Dursley, Coleford, Newnham, Stow-on-the-Wold and Campden.

3rd Volunteer Battalion.
Formed in July, 1900, the Regiment's 3rd Volunteer Battalion comprised headquarters and eight companies at Bristol.

Uniform
Both the 1st and 2nd Volunteer Battalions had green uniforms, the latter having scarlet facings. When the 3rd was formed the uniform adopted was khaki with scarlet facings.

Territorial Force
In 1908 the 1st, 2nd and 3rd Volunteer Battalions formed the Regiment's 4th, 5th and 6th Battalion (TF) in order of seniority.

26. Captain (Hon. Major) J.H. Woodward, 1st Gloucestershire Rifle Volunteer Corps.

WORCESTERSHIRE REGIMENT

Prior to 1881 the line, militia and volunteers of the Counties of Worcestershire and Herefordshire comprised Number 22 Sub-District. The reorganisations of that year saw the militia and volunteers of the latter county removed, the remaining units then forming the Worcestershire Regiment — 1st Battalion (late 29th Foot), 2nd Battalion (late 36th Foot), 3rd and 4th Battalions (Worcestershire Militia) and the 1st and 2nd Worcestershire Rifle Volunteer Corps.

1st Volunteer Battalion. "SOUTH AFRICA 1900-01"

The senior company of the Battalion was formed in 1859 and in 1860 this, with other rifle corps from the County was organised as the 1st Administrative Battalion of Worcestershire Rifle Volunteers. Consolidated as 1st Worcestershire Rifle Volunteer Corps in 1880, the Battalion comprised of eleven companies located as follows — Wolverley, Tenbury, Kidderminster (3), Bewdley, Halesowen, Dudley, Stourport, Stourbridge and Oldbury. Headquarters were at Hagley.

In 1882 a new company was raised at Dudley and in the following year the Corps was designated as 1st Volunteer Battalion, The Worcestershire Regiment. Battalion Headquarters moved to Stourbridge between 1885-86 and then to Kidderminster by 1891.

2nd Volunteer Battalion. "SOUTH AFRICA 1900-02"

The 2nd Volunteer Battalion of the Regiment was formerly the 2nd Worcestershire Rifle Volunteer Corps, its senior company dating from 1860 and the Corps as a whole existing prior to 1880 as the County's 2nd Administrative Battalion. Headquarters of the 2nd Corps were at Worcester and its eight company establishment was located at Worcester (2), Gt. Malvern, Evesham, Droitwich, Pershore, Bromsgrove and Redditch.

Designation as 2nd Volunteer Battalion was notified in General Order 80 of June, 1883. An additional company was sanctioned in 1900 but this was short lived and was broken up by 1905.

Uniform
Both battalions were dressed in rifle green uniforms, the 1st adopting black facings in 1904.

Territorial Force
In 1908 both battalions transferred to the Territorial Force, forming the Regiment's 7th and 8th Battalions respectively.

27. Members of the 2nd Volunteer Battalion, Worcestershire Regiment after a presentation of Volunteer Long Service Medals in 1895. (Worcestershire Regiment Museum)

28. Colonel M.S. Brownrigg (Officer Commanding Regimental District No. 30) with officers, N.C.Os and Sergeant Instructor, Stonyhurst College Cadet Corps. Affiliated to 1st Volunteer Battalion, East Lancashire Regiment.

EAST LANCASHIRE REGIMENT

The Regiment was formed out of the several battalions comprising Number 15 Sub-District Brigade — 1st Battalion (late 30th Foot), 2nd Battalion (late 59th Foot), 3rd Battalion (late 5th Royal Lancashire Militia) and the 2nd and 3rd Lancashire Rifle Volunteer Corps. The volunteers assumed the title of the Regiment in 1889.

1st Volunteer Battalion. "SOUTH AFRICA 1900-02"
In 1880 the 8th Admin. Battalion of Lancashire Rifle Volunteers (senior corps formed in 1859) was consolidated as the County's 2nd Corps. Headquarters were at Blackburn and the Battalion's original ten companies were located at Blackburn (6), Over Darwen (2) and Clitheroe (2). In the last year of the Volunteer movement the strength of the Battalion was returned as 880 all ranks.

2nd Volunteer Battalion. "SOUTH AFRICA 1900-02"
This battalion was previously the 3rd Lancashire Rifle Volunteer Corps and before that the County's 3rd Admin. Battalion (senior corps formed in 1859). With headquarters in Burnley the Battalion's original twelve companies were located at Burnley (4), Padiham, Accrington (3), Haslington, Ramsbottom, Stackshead and Lytham. Some 1,057 all ranks were recorded in the Battalion's last return made in 1907.

Uniform
Both battalions wore scarlet, the 1st with white facings and the 2nd with black.

Territorial Force
The 4th and 5th Battalions (TF) were formed in 1908 by the 1st and 2nd Volunteer Battalions respectively.

EAST SURREY REGIMENT

The East Surrey Regiment was formed in 1881 out of the several battalions comprising Number 47 Sub-District Brigade — 1st Battalion (late 31st Foot), 2nd Battalion (late 70th Foot), 3rd Battalion (late 1st Royal Surrey Militia), 4th Battalion (late 3rd Royal Surrey Militia) and the Surrey Rifle Volunteer corps numbered 1st, 3rd, 5th and 7th. Three of the volunteer corps adopted the title of the Regiment in 1887, but one, the 1st, retained its designation up to 1908.

1st Surrey (South London) Volunteer Rifle Corps. "SOUTH AFRICA 1900-02"

The senior rifle corps in Surrey was formed in 1859 at Camberwell and served as the Regiment's 1st Volunteer Battalion (eight companies) between 1881-1908.

2nd Volunteer Battalion. "SOUTH AFRICA 1900-02"

Upon consolidation in 1880, the 1st Administrative Battalion of Surrey Rifle Volunteers assumed the number of its senior corps — 4th. However, by September this had been changed to 3rd. The original headquarters of the 3rd Surrey Corps were at Clapham Park and its six companies located at Brixton (2), Carshalton, Wimbledon (2) and Epsom. In 1894 headquarters were moved to Wimbledon, two years later two new companies were sanctioned and in 1900 additional personnel brought the establishment of the Battalion up to ten companies. By 1904 a certain amount of reorganisation had taken place within the Battalion, its ten companies at that time being located — Streatham (2), Sutton (2), Wimbledon (4) and Epsom (2). Further changes saw the Battalion in 1907 situated — Streatham (2), Sutton (2), Wimbledon (3), Epsom, Putney and Leatherhead. Its returned strength at that time being 575 all ranks.

29. Silver pouch belt plate 3rd Volunteer Battalion, East Surrey Regiment.

3rd Volunteer Battalion. "SOUTH AFRICA 1900-02"
Previously the 5th Surrey Rifle Volunteer Corps, and before that the County's 2nd Administrative Battalion, the Battalion's original establishment was eight companies — Esher, Richmond (2), Kingston (4) and Chertsey. Headquarters were in Kingston and in 1900 two additional companies were sanctioned at Egham and Richmond.

4th Volunteer Battalion. "SOUTH AFRICA 1900-02"
In 1880 two Surrey corps were amalgamated as 7th Corps comprising — headquarters at Southwark and ten companies. These were the 7th (six companies at Southwark) and the 26th consisting of four companies from Lavender Hill, Clapham. Shortly after amalgamation headquarters were given in the Army List as being at Upper Kennington Lane. This was changed in 1902 when new premises were taken over at St John's Hill, Clapham Junction. A cyclist company was formed at headquarters in 1900 and the Battalion's last recorded strength was 930 all ranks.

Uniform
Only two battalions, the 2nd with green in 1897, and the 4th, green/scarlet in 1889, adopted the scarlet with white facings uniform of the East Surrey Regiment. Both the 1st Surrey Volunteer Rifle Corps and 3rd Volunteer Battalion retaining their green with scarlet facings through till 1908.

Territorial Force
In 1908 the Regiment's two Territorial battalions — 5th and 6th, were provided by the 2nd and 3rd Volunteer Battalions. The 1st Surrey and the 4th Volunteer Battalion both joined the London Regiment, forming its 21st and 23rd Battalions respectively.

DUKE OF CORNWALL'S LIGHT INFANTRY

Prior to 1881, Number 35 Sub-District comprised the 32nd and 46th Regiments of Foot, the Royal Cornwall Rangers Militia and the 1st and 2nd Cornwall Rifle Volunteer Corps. In the reorganisations of that year, these battalions became the Duke of Cornwall's Light Infantry.

1st Volunteer Battalion. "SOUTH AFRICA 1900-01"
The 1st Administrative Battalion of Cornwall Rifle Volunteers was formed at Penzance in 1860, its component companies being the corps from the western half of the County. In 1880 the Battalion was consolidated as the 1st Cornwall (Duke of

30. 2nd Volunteer Battalion, Duke of Cornwall's Light Infantry. Quartermaster Sergeant Burns, one of the Battalion's best shots, at Bisley c1890. (Army Museums Ogilby Trust)

Cornwall's) Rifle Volunteer Corps. The new Corps had its first headquarters at Penzance, but within a year a move was made to Falmouth, and then in 1902, new premises were found at Truro.

Eleven companies — Penzance, Camborne, Falmouth, Helston, Truro (2), Hayle, Redruth, Trelowarren, St Just and Penryn was the establishment of the 1st Volunteer Battalion (designated in 1885) until 1900 when an additional two were sanctioned.

2nd Volunteer Battalion. "SOUTH AFRICA 1900-01"
In 1860 rifle corps formed in the eastern half of Cornwall were formed into an admin. battalion. The senior corps of this formation was numbered 4th and consequently, upon the consolidation of the Battalion in 1880, the new corps received the same number. By the end of the year, however, this had been changed to 2nd, its full title being — 2nd Cornwall (Duke of Cornwall's) Rifle Volunteer Corps.

Headquarters of the 2nd Volunteer Battalion (redesignated 1885) were at Bodmin and its original nine companies were located — Liskeard, Callington, Launceston, St. Austell, Bodmin, Wadebridge, St Columb, Camelford and Saltash. Two new companies were sanctioned during the Boer War and this remained the establishment of the battalion until 1908.

Uniform
Dark grey uniforms with scarlet facings were worn by the 1st Volunteer Battalion through to 1908. The 2nd wore scarlet with white facings.

Territorial Force
In 1908 both battalions were combined to form the Regiment's 4th and 5th Battalions (TF).

DUKE OF WELLINGTON'S (WEST RIDING REGIMENT)

This regiment was formed out of the several units comprising Number 9 Sub-District prior to the reorganisations of 1881. These were — 33rd Foot (1st Bn), 76th Foot (2nd Bn) and 6th West York Militia (3rd and 4th Bns). Number 9 Sub-District Brigade also included two volunteer corps, the 4th and 6th Yorkshire (West Riding). To these were added by the end of 1881 the 9th Yorkshire (West Riding). The Regiment's volunteer corps were redesignated as volunteer battalions in 1883.

1st Volunteer Battalion. "SOUTH AFRICA 1900-02"
In 1860 four companies of rifle volunteers that had been formed in Halifax the previous year were amalgamated as one corps. As the 4th Yorkshire (West Riding) Rifle Volunteer Corps the Halifax volunteers were later increased by four companies. However, the establishment was later reduced to six — Halifax (4) Brighouse and Cleckheaton.

2nd Volunteer Battalion. "SOUTH AFRICA 1900-02"
In 1862 the 5th Administrative Battalion of Yorkshire (West Riding) Rifle Volunteers was formed out of a number of corps from around the Huddersfield area. This battalion, in 1880, was consolidated as 6th Corps, its establishment at this time being ten companies — Huddersfield (4), Holmfirth, Saddleworth (4) and Mirfield.

31. Officers' pouch belt plate, 4th Yorkshire (West Riding) Rifle Volunteers. (J. Byrne)

3rd Volunteer Battalion. "SOUTH AFRICA 1900-02"

The 3rd Volunteer Battalion, Duke of Wellington's Regiment had its headquarters at Skipton-in-Craven where, in 1860, several corps were organised into the 2nd Administrative Battalion of Yorkshire (West Riding) Rifle Volunteers. Consolidated as 9th Corps in 1880, the Battalion was for a short time included in the West Yorkshire Regiment. It had previously formed part of Number 10 Sub-District and was part of that formation's volunteer line-up. By the beginning of 1882, however, the 9th had transferred to the Duke of Wellington's.

The battalion's original eight companies were located at Skipton-in-Craven, Settle, Burley, Keighley (3), Haworth and Bingley. Additional companies were sanctioned in 1884 (1) and 1900 (2) and at the end of 1907 the strength of the battalion stood at 1,198 all ranks.

Uniform

By 1889 all three battalions are recorded in the Army List as wearing scarlet uniforms with white facings. Prior to that, however, the 1st and 2nd are shown as having sky blue facings, while the 3rd had buff.

Territorial Force

Transfer to the Territorial Force saw 1st Volunteer Battalion as 4th Battalion, the 2nd and 5th as 7th and the 3rd as 6th.

BORDER REGIMENT

The Border Regiment comprised the several units that prior to the reorganisations of 1881 constituted Number 2 Sub-District Brigade — 34th Foot (1st Bn), 55th Foot (2nd Bn), Royal Cumberland Militia (3rd Bn) and Royal Westmorland Militia (4th Bn). The volunteers from the Counties of Cumberland and Westmorland also joined the Regiment, and these, in 1887, assumed the titles of 1st (Cumberland) and 2nd (Westmorland) Volunteer Battalions.

1st (Cumberland) Volunteer Battalion. "SOUTH AFRICA 1900-02"

By the end of 1860 the eleven rifle corps formed throughout Cumberland had been organised into the County's 1st Admin. Battalion. In 1880 the Battalion was consolidated to form the 1st Cumberland Rifle Volunteer Corps, comprising headquarters at Keswick and thirteen companies located —Carlisle

(3), Whitehaven, Keswick, Brampton, Penrith (2), Alston, Workington, Cockermouth, Egremont and Wigton. In 1896 Battalion Headquarters were moved to Carlisle.

As a result of the War in South Africa recruiting within the County was such that an additional three companies were formed. These, however, did not join the Battalion but instead, together with the Whitehaven, Workington, Cockermouth, Egremont and Wigton companies formed a new battalion designated as 3rd (Cumberland). The 1st (Cumberland) Volunteer Battalion retained its eight companies until 1908, its last return recording a strength of 527 all ranks.

2nd (Westmorland) Volunteer Battalion.
"SOUTH AFRICA 1900-02"
The Battalion was previously the 1st Westmorland Rifle Volunteer Corps, and before that the County's 1st Admin. Battalion which had been formed in 1860. In 1881 the strength of the Battalion stood at nine companies — Kirkby Lonsdale, Appleby, Kendal (3), Staveley, Windermere, Ambleside and Grasmere. Headquarters were in Kendal and the nine company establishment was maintained until transfer to the Territorial Force in 1908.

32. Officers' helmet plate, 1st Volunteer Battalion, Border Regiment.

3rd (Cumberland) Volunteer Battalion.
"SOUTH AFRICA 1900-02"
As previously mentioned, this battalion was formed in 1900 by withdrawing from the 1st (Cumberland) Volunteer Battalion its Whitehaven, Workington, Cockermouth, Egremont and Wigton Companies. To these five companies a further three, newly raised, were added at Workington, Frizington and Aspatria. Headquarters were placed at Workington and the eight company establishment remained until 1908.

Uniform
All three battalions wore scarlet uniforms with white facings. The 2nd (Westmorland) Volunteer Battalion, however, originally had green facings; the change being indicated in the Army List during 1888.

Territorial Force
In 1908 the 1st and 2nd Volunteer Battalions were merged to form the Regiment's 4th Battalion (TF) while the 3rd Volunteer Battalion provided its 5th.

ROYAL SUSSEX REGIMENT

The Royal Sussex Regiment was formed out of Number 43 Sub-District — 1st Battalion (late 35th Foot), 2nd Battalion (late 107th Foot), 3rd and 4th Battalions (late Royal Sussex Militia). The Regiment also included three volunteer battalions.

1st Volunteer Battalion. "SOUTH AFRICA 1900-02"
The 1st Sussex Rifle Volunteer Corps was formed at Brighton in 1859. It maintained six companies until 1886 when an additional two were sanctioned. The establishment was again raised in 1900, this time by one company. The designation — 1st Volunteer Battalion, Royal Sussex Regiment was assumed in 1887.

2nd Volunteer Battalion. "SOUTH AFRICA 1900-02"
In 1880 the 1st Administrative Battalion of Sussex Rifle Volunteers, containing many corps that had been formed during 1859-60, wasx consolidated as the 2nd Sussex Rifle Volunteer Corps. At the time of formation, the new corps had its headquarters at Worthing and an establishment of eleven companies — Cuckfield (2), East Grinstead, Petworth, Horsham, Arundel, Chichester, Worthing, Westbourne, Hurstpierpoint and Henfield. The title of the Regiment was assumed in 1887 and an additional company sanctioned in 1900.

33. Members of "L" (Henfield) Company, 2nd Volunteer Battalion, Royal Sussex Regiment. (John Woodroff)

1st Cinque Ports Volunteer Rifle Corps.
"SOUTH AFRICA 1900-02"
Upon consolidation as the 1st Cinque Ports Rifle Volunteer Corps in 1880, the 1st Cinque Ports Administrative Battalion comprised the old 1st Corps (formed in 1859) together with the 4th Sussex. Although provision had been made for a corps of six companies, only four — Hastings, Battle, Ticehurst and Lewes were set up in 1880. By 1885, however, sufficient personnel had been recruited at Rye and Hastings to complete establishment. With the addition of new companies at Rotherfield (1891), Ore (1895), Hastings and Ore (1900) the strength of the 1st Cinque Ports in 1908 stood at ten companies.

Uniform
Both the Sussex battalions wore scarlet uniforms with blue facings. The Cinque Ports Volunteers changed from grey to blue in 1898, but in this case the blue was lighter than that worn by the Royal Sussex Regiment.

Territorial Force
In 1908 the 1st Volunteer Battalion was converted to part of 1st Home Counties Brigade, Royal Field Artillery. Both the 2nd Volunteer Battalion and 1st Cinque Ports Volunteer Rifle Corps remained as part of the Regiment, forming its 4th and 5th Battalions (TF) respectively.

HAMPSHIRE REGIMENT

The Hampshire Regiment was formerly Number 40 Sub-District Brigade — 1st Battalion (late 37th Foot), 2nd Battalion late 67th Foot) and 3rd Battalion (late Hampshire Militia). The volunteers were provided by the 1st, 2nd, 3rd Hampshire and the 1st Isle of Wight Corps. These all assumed the title of the Regiment in 1885.

1st Volunteer Battalion. "SOUTH AFRICA 1900-02"
The senior company of the 1st Volunteer Battalion dates from 1859 and together with other corps formed the 1st Administrative Battalion of Hampshire Rifle Volunteers. In 1880 the 1st Admin. Battalion was consolidated as the County's 1st Corps, its headquarters being at Winchester and a ten company establishment located — Winchester (3), Botley, Romsey, Andover, Hartley Wintney, Alresford, Alton and Basingstoke.

In 1884 a new company was sanctioned and subsequently formed at St Mary's College, Winchester. This was followed in 1899 by another at Aldershot and then in 1892 the Battalion's establishment was raised to thirteen companies when a new detachment was created at Stockbridge. A further five companies were added as a result of the increase in volunteers during the Boer War.

2nd Volunteer Battalion. "SOUTH AFRICA 1900-02"
This battalion (senior company formed in 1860) was formerly the 2nd Hampshire Rifle Volunteer Corps and before that the County's 4th Administrative Battalion. Upon consolidation in 1880, the nine companies of the 2nd Corps were located — Southampton (4), Lymington, Christchurch, Lyndhurst and Bournemouth (2). Headquarters were at Southampton.

By 1883 the establishment of the Corps had reached twelve companies, but in 1885 this was reduced to eight when four companies were detached to form the 4th Hampshire Rifle Volunteers. According to the regimental history of the Royal Hampshire Regiment, the companies removed were those at Bournemouth, Christchurch, Lymington and Ringwood. This would suggest that one of the original Bournemouth Companies had been transferred to Ringwood. A new company was added in 1900.

34. Officer, 1st Volunteer Battalion, Hampshire Regiment. (John Woodroff)

3rd (Duke of Connaught's Own) Volunteer Battalion. "SOUTH AFRICA 1900-02"

In 1880 the 2nd Administrative Battalion of Hampshire Rifle Volunteers (senior company formed in 1860) was consolidated as 3rd Corps. Headquarters were in Portsmouth and the Battalion's original eleven companies were located — Portsmouth (5), Gosport (2), Havant, Petersfield, Fareham and Porchester.

The Corps was redesignated as 3rd Volunteer Battalion in 1885, adding "Duke of Connaught's Own" to its title eight years later upon the occasion of His Royal Highness becoming Hon Colonel. A new company was added in 1884 followed by six more in 1900.

4th Volunteer Battalion. "SOUTH AFRICA 1900-02"

The 4th Hampshire Rifle Volunteer Corps was formed in April 1885 from the Bournemouth, Christchurch, Lymington and Ringwood Companies of the 2nd Corps. Headquarters were placed at Bournemouth and the establishment set at six companies. By 1900 there were eleven companies, one being mounted and known locally as the New Forest Scouts.

5th (Isle of Wight, "Princess Beatrice's") Volunteer Battalion. "SOUTH AFRICA 1900-01"

The senior company of the 1st Isle of Wight Rifle Volunteers was formed in 1860 and together with all other corps raised on the Island joined the 1st Administrative Battalion. Consolidated as 1st Corps in 1880, the Battalion comprised headquarters at Newport and eight companies — Ryde (2), Newport (2), Nunwell, Ventnor (2) and Cowes. A cyclist company was formed and added at Newport in 1900.

Uniform

The four Hampshire battalions all wore scarlet with white facings, the 1st changing from black facings in 1882 while the other three all began with yellow. A green uniform was worn by the 5th Volunteer Battalion.

Territorial Force

The 1st to 4th Volunteer Battalions provided the Regiment's 4th to 7th Battalions (TF) in order of seniority. The 5th became the 8th Battalion.

35. Bandsman 1st Volunteer Battalion, South Staffordshire Regiment. (Chris Coogan)

SOUTH STAFFORDSHIRE REGIMENT

In 1881 Number 19 Sub-District Brigade provided the units for the South Staffordshire Regiment — 1st Battalion (late 38th Foot), 2nd Battalion (late 80th Foot), 3rd and 4th Battalions (late 1st King's Own Stafford Militia). The original volunteers were the 2nd and 5th Staffordshire Rifle Volunteer Corps, but these were exchanged in 1882 for the 1st, 3rd and 4th Corps, then attached to the North Staffordshire Regiment.

1st Volunteer Battalion. "SOUTH AFRICA 1900-02"
The 1st Volunteer Battalion was previously the 1st Staffordshire Rifle Volunteer Corps and prior to that the County's 3rd Administrative Battalion. Upon consolidation in 1880 battalion headquarters were at Handsworth and eight companies were located at — Handsworth (2), Brierley, Kingswinford (soon moved to Wordsley), West Bromwich, Seisdon (later Sutton Coldfield), Patshull and Smethwick. Additions were made to the Battalion when in 1900 new companies were formed at West Bromwich and Smethwick, and in the following year Handsworth provided a company of cyclists. Later a reduction in establishment to ten companies was made and after a number of re-locations these were situated — Handsworth (3), Brierley (2), West Bromwich (2), Sutton Coldfield and Smethwick (2).

2nd Volunteer Battalion. "SOUTH AFRICA 1900-02"
When the 5th Administrative Battalion of Staffordshire Rifle Volunteers was consolidated in 1880 it assumed the number of its senior corps — 4th. This was changed to 3rd, however, before the end of the year — corps headquarters being at Walsall and a six company establishment located at — Walsall (2), Bloxwich, Brownhills, Cannock and Wednesbury.

Two new companies were formed at Walsall and Wednesbury in 1884. In the same year the headquarters of the Cannock Company ('E') were moved to Brownhills. However, before 1901 this was disbanded and reformed at Walsall. The last addition to the 2nd Volunteer Battalion was in 1901 when 'I' Company was formed at Walsall.

3rd Volunteer Battalion. "SOUTH AFRICA 1900-02"
The 4th Administrative Battalion of Staffordshire Rifle Volunteers was formed at Wolverhampton in 1860 and in 1880 was consolidated as 5th, later, 4th Corps. Originally comprising twelve companies — Wolverhampton (6), Willenhall, Tipton, Sedgley, Bilston (2) and Tettenhall, the Battalion added one more at Wolverhampton in 1900. That same year the headquarters of 'H' Company were moved from Bilston to Darlaston. In 1906 a reduction in establishment brought the

strength of the 3rd Volunteer Battalion down to nine companies, their locations after several mergers and disbandments being — Wolverhampton (5), Willenhall, Sedgley, Bilston and Tettenhall.

Uniform
Two of the Regiment's volunteer battalions, 1st and 2nd, had scarlet uniforms with white facings. The 3rd also wore scarlet, but with black collars and cuffs.

Territorial Force
In 1908 most of the 1st Volunteer Battalion transferred to the 1st North Midland Field Company, Royal Engineers. The Handsworth companies merged with those of the 2nd Volunteer Battalion, and together formed the Regiment's 5th Battalion (TF). The 3rd Volunteer Battalion became the 6th Battalion, South Staffordshire Regiment.

DORSETSHIRE REGIMENT

The Dorsetshire Regiment was formed in 1881 out of the several units (less the 75th Regiment) then comprising Number 39 Sub-District. The 54th Regiment was added to make up the regular battalions and with the Dorsetshire Militia and Rifle Volunteers, the Regiment was organised — 1st Battalion (late 39th Foot), 2nd Battalion (late 54th Foot), 3rd Battalion (late Dorsetshire Militia) and 1st Dorsetshire Rifle Volunteer Corps. The volunteers assumed the title of the Regiment in 1887.

1st Volunteer Battalion. "SOUTH AFRICA 1900-01"
The first of twelve rifle corps was formed at Bridport in 1859 and these were later organised into an administrative battalion, and in 1880, one corps titled 1st Dorsetshire Rifle Volunteers. The several companies comprising the Battalion were scattered around the County — Bridport, Wareham, Dorchester, Poole, Weymouth, Wimborne, Sherborne, Blandford, Shaftesbury, Stalbridge and Gillingham. Headquarters were in Dorchester.

Uniform
Green uniforms with scarlet facings had been introduced into the 1st Admin. Battalion upon its formation in 1860. These colours were maintained and were still being worn upon transfer to the Territorial Force in 1908.

36. Members of "F" Company (Wimborne), 1st Volunteer Battalion, Dorsetshire Regiment who volunteered for active service in South Africa. (Dorset Military Museum)

Territorial Force
The 1st Volunteer Battalion provided the Regiment's 4th Battalion (TF) in 1908.

PRINCE OF WALES'S VOLUNTEERS (SOUTH LANCASHIRE REGIMENT)

The Regiment was formed out of the units comprising Number 14 Sub-District Brigade — 1st Battalion (late 40th Foot), 2nd Battalion (late 82nd Foot), 3rd Battalion (late 4th Royal Lancashire Militia) and the 9th and 21st Lancashire Rifle Volunteer Corps. The volunteers assumed the title of the Regiment in 1886.

1st Volunteer Battalion. "SOUTH AFRICA 1900-02"
In 1880 the 9th Lancashire Rifle Volunteer Corps (formed at Warrington in 1859) and the 49th Lancashire Rifle Volunteer Corps (formed at Newton-le-Willows in 1860) were amalgamated as 9th Corps. Headquarters were placed at Warrington and seven companies were located — six at Warrington and one at Newton-le-Willows. During 1900-1903 additional companies were sanctioned bringing the establishment of the Battalion up to eleven.

2nd Volunteer Battalion. "SOUTH AFRICA 1900-01"
The 21st Lancashire Rifle Volunteer Corps was formed in 1880 by the amalgamation of the 47th Corps (formed at St Helens in 1860) and the 48th Corps (formed at Prescot in 1860). Headquarters of the Battalion were at St Helens and its strength ten companies — St Helens (9) Prescot (1).

Uniform
The 1st Volunteer Battalion wore scarlet uniforms with green facings, changing to white facings in 1890. In the 2nd their green with scarlet facings was retained through to 1908.

Territorial Force
The Regiment's 4th and 5th Battalions (TF) were formed by the 1st and 2nd Volunteer Battalions respectively.

37. 2nd Volunteer Battalion, The Prince of Wales's Volunteers (South Lancashire Regiment).

WELSH REGIMENT

The Welsh Regiment was formed out of the several regiments comprising Number 24 Sub-District Brigade — 1st Battalion (late 41st Foot), 2nd Battalion (late 69th Foot) and 3rd Battalion (late Royal Glamorgan Militia). The volunteers — one corps from Pembrokeshire and two from Glamorganshire, assumed the title of the Regiment in 1887, and one other, the 3rd Glamorgan, retained its rifle volunteer designation.

1st (Pembrokeshire) Volunteer Battalion.
"SOUTH AFRICA 1900-02"

The 1st Administrative Battalion of Pembrokeshire Rifle Volunteers (senior company formed in 1859) also included corps from outside of the County and upon consolidation as 1st Corps in 1880 assumed the title — 1st Pembrokeshire Rifle Volunteer Corps (Pembroke, Carmarthen, Cardigan and Haverfordwest). Headquarters of the corps were at Haverfordwest and its original ten companies were located — Milford, Haverfordwest (3), Pembroke, Cardigan, Llandeilo, Carmarthen (2) and Llanelly. Two additional companies were sanctioned and added in 1900.

2nd Volunteer Battalion. "SOUTH AFRICA 1900-02"

In March 1880 the 1st Administrative Battalion of Glamorganshire Rifle Volunteers (senior company formed in 1859) was consolidated as the county's 1st Corps. At this time the Battalion's twelve companies were located — Margam (2), Swansea (3), Taibach (2), Cwm Avon, Bridgend, Neath (2) and Cowbridge. Headquarters were moved from Margan to Bridgend in 1896.

When the Corps assumed the Welsh Regiment title in 1887 it was listed as 2nd (Glamorgan) Volunteer Battalion. However, the sub-title was not shown in the Army List after December 1888.

In 1905 three of the Battalion's companies were transferred to the 3rd Glamorgan at Swansea, while at the same time personnel from around the Cardiff area were absorbed from the 3rd Volunteer Battalion. This was to bring the establishment of the 2nd Volunteer Battalion up to fourteen companies with headquarters in Cardiff.

3rd Volunteer Battalion. "SOUTH AFRICA 1900-02"

This battalion dates from 1859 and was one of the strongest in the British Isles. In 1880 the 2nd Administrative Battalion of Glamorganshire Rifle Volunteers was consolidated as the County's 2nd Corps of twenty-two companies — Dowlais (2), Mountain Ash (3), Cardiff (7), Merthyr Tydfil (4), Taff's Well

38. Sergeant E.R. McGregor, 3rd Volunteer Battalion, Welsh Regiment. (Welsh Regiment Museum)

(2), Aberdare (2), Pontypridd and Hirwaun. Headquarters were in Cardiff.

Under General Order 181 of December 1887, the 2nd corps became the 3rd (Glamorgan) Volunteer Battalion of the Welsh Regiment. The sub-title was later removed and was last seen in the Army List for February 1891.

By 1900 the Battalion's establishment stood at twenty-four companies, which in 1905 was reduced to fifteen after personnel from the Cardiff area were transferred to the 2nd Volunteer Battalion. At the same time, Battalion Headquarters were moved to Pontypridd.

3rd Glamorganshire Volunteer Battalion.
"SOUTH AFRICA 1900-02"

The 3rd Corps was formed at Swansea in 1859. It maintained six companies until 1900, when three more were added, and from 1905, twelve companies after personnel from the 2nd Volunteer Battalion were transferred.

Uniform
All four battalions wore the Regiment's scarlet with white facings, the 1st, 2nd and 3rd originally wearing blue facings, and the 3rd Glamorgan — green.

Territorial Force
The 1st and 3rd Volunteer Battalions, together with the 3rd Glamorgan became the Regiment's 4th, 5th and 6th Battalions (TF) respectively. Some members of the 2nd Volunteer Battalion joined the 7th Battalion, but the majority were transferred to the Royal Artillery.

BLACK WATCH (ROYAL HIGHLANDERS)

The two Line battalions of this regiment were formed from the 42nd and 73rd Regiments of Foot; the 3rd Battalion came from the Royal Perth Militia and the six battalions of volunteers were provided by the Counties of Forfarshire, Perthshire and Fifeshire. These assumed the title of the Regiment in 1887.

1st (City of Dundee) Volunteer Battalion.
"SOUTH AFRICA 1900-02"
Formed in Dundee in 1859 as the 1st Forfarshire Rifle Volunteer Corps. When the 1st Volunteer Battalion title was assumed in 1887 the sub-title was listed as "Dundee". However, by 1891, this appeared in the Army List as "City of Dundee". The strength of the Battalion was originally eight companies, an additional two being formed during 1900.

2nd (Angus) Volunteer Battalion.
"SOUTH AFRICA 1900-02"
In 1880 the 1st Administrative Battalion of Forfarshire Rifle Volunteers was consolidated as 2nd Corps, its headquarters being at Friockheim with an establishment of fourteen companies — Forfar (2), Arbroath (4), Montrose (2), Brechin (2), Newtyle, Glamis, Kirriemuir and Friockheim. Headquarters were moved to Arbroath in 1887 and in 1894 two companies were lost when 'F' at Arbroath was disbanded and 'L' (Newtyle) and 'M' (Glamis) were amalgamated.

3rd (Dundee Highland) Volunteer Battalion.
"SOUTH AFRICA 1900-02"
Both the 10th (formed 1860) and the 14th (formed 1861) Forfarshire Rifle Volunteer Corps were from Dundee and in 1868 were amalgamated as a single corps of six companies titled — 10th Forfarshire (Dundee Highland). This title was changed to 3rd Corps in 1880 and in 1900 two additional companies were sanctioned.

4th (Perthshire) Volunteer Battalion.
"SOUTH AFRICA 1900-02"
The 1st Administrative Battalion of Perthshire Rifle Volunteers was consolidated as 1st Corps in 1880. Headquarters were at Perth and the new corps comprised seven companies located at Perth (3), Dunblane, Crieff, Doune and Auchterarder. Authority to form a new company at Bridge of Allan was received in 1885. In 1900 another three were sanctioned, but these were disbanded; one in 1902 and two in 1905.

39. Officers' helmet plate, 3rd Forfarshire (Dundee Highland) Rifle Volunteer Corps.

5th (Perthshire Highland) Volunteer Battalion.
"SOUTH AFRICA 1900-02"
When the 2nd Administrative Battalion of Perthshire Rifle Volunteers was consolidated in 1880 as 2nd Corps its organisation was — Headquarters Birnam and eight companies located at Aberfeldy, Killin, Blairgowrie, Coupar Angus, Alyth, St Martin's, Birnam and Pitlochry. In 1899 headquarters of 'F' (St Martin's) Company were moved to New Stone. That same year two new companies were formed, one each at Blairgowrie and Birnam, but these were disbanded in 1904 and 1905 respectively.

6th (Fifeshire) Volunteer Battalion.
"SOUTH AFRICA 1900-02"
This battalion was formerly the 1st Fifeshire Rifle Volunteer Corps, and before that the 1st Administrative Battalion of Fifeshire Rifle Volunteers. With headquarters in St Andrews, the Battalion's original twelve companies were located at Dumfermline (2), Cupar (2), East Anstruther, Colinsburgh, St Andrews, Leslie, Falkland, Kirkcaldy, Lochgelly and Newburgh.

Before transfer to the Territorial Force in 1908 the following changes in battalion organisation took place — in 1900 the two Cupar companies ("C & D") were moved to Kirkcaldy while at the same time 'K' (Kirkcaldy) moved to Cupar. A cyclist company was formed at Dumfermline in 1901 and in 1906, 'F' Company at Colinsburgh moved to Levan.

Uniform
The uniform of the six volunteer battalions was as follows:- 1st V.B: scarlet tunics with blue facings, 2nd V.B: scarlet tunics with blue facings changing to doublets and Black Watch trews in 1882, 3rd V.B: scarlet doublets with blue facings, Black Watch kilts changing to trews in 1882, 4th V.B: grey with scarlet facings changing to scarlet doublets, blue facings and Black Watch trews in 1883 — kilts from 1901, 5th V.B: dark grey doublets, scarlet facings, Black Watch kilts, 6th V.B: scarlet tunics, blue facings.

Territorial Force
The transfer to the Territorial Force in 1908 went as follows:- 1st V.B. as 4th Bn., 2nd and 3rd V.Bs amalgamated as 5th Bn., 4th V.B. as 6th Bn., 6th V.B. as 7th Bn. The 5th V.B. was originally to form the 8th Black Watch. However, this battalion was not found and instead the 5th V.B. became the Highland Cyclist Battalion.

OXFORDSHIRE LIGHT INFANTRY

Prior to the reorganisations of 1881, Number 42 Sub-District comprised the 52nd and 85th Regiments of Foot and the militia and volunteers of the Counties of Buckinghamshire and Oxfordshire. When the Oxfordshire Light Infantry was formed the 85th Foot became 2nd Battalion, King's (Shropshire Light Infantry), its place then being taken, as 1st Battalion, by the 43rd Regiment.

1st (Oxford University) Volunteer Battalion.
This battalion was formed at the University in 1859. Its title, 1st Oxfordshire Rifle Volunteer Corps was changed to 1st (Oxford University) Volunteer Battalion, Oxfordshire Light Infantry in 1887. There were six companies.

2nd Volunteer Battalion. "SOUTH AFRICA 1900-01"
In 1875 the several Oxfordshire rifle corps, formed since 1860 outside the University, were consolidated as the 2nd Oxfordshire Rifle Volunteer Corps. With headquarters in Oxford, the Corps was designated as 2nd Volunteer Battalion in 1887. Its original establishment of six companies — Oxford, Banbury, Henley, Deddington, Thame and Woodstock, was increased by one in 1884, and then by two during the war in South Africa.

1st Bucks Volunteer Rifle Corps.
"SOUTH AFRICA 1900-02"
The 1st Bucks Rifle Volunteer Corps was formed at Great Marlow in 1859 and in 1875 merged with other Buckinghamshire corps to form a battalion of five companies — Great Marlow, Buckingham, Aylesbury, Slough and Eton College. In 1878 the College personnel left the Battalion to form their own unit. Soon, other detachments were raised at High Wycombe, Buckingham and Wolverton, and by 1881 the establishment of the 1st Bucks stood at seven companies.

Although ranked as 3rd Volunteer Battalion, the 1st Bucks did not assume any change in designation. Its establishment was increased to eight companies in 1882 and then to nine in 1900.

2nd Bucks (Eton College) Volunteer Rifle Corps.
In 1878 it was decided that the Eton College elements of the 1st Bucks Rifle Volunteer Corps should be detached to form their own corps. This was carried out and on 15th June the first officers were gazetted to the 2nd Bucks (Eton College) Rifle Volunteers. Under General Order 181 of December 1887, the Corps was redesignated as 4th (Eton College) Volunteer Battalion of the Oxfordshire Light Infantry. However, in 1902 the title reverted to 2nd Bucks. The establishment of the

Battalion was increased from four to five companies in 1900.

Uniform

The Oxfordshire battalions both wore scarlet, the 1st with dark blue facings and the 2nd with white. In Buckinghamshire, the 1st Corps had dark grey uniforms with scarlet facings while the College chose a lighter shade of grey and with light blue facings.

Territorial Force

In 1908 only two battalions remained with the Regiment, the 2nd forming the 4th Battalion (TF) while the 1st Bucks became known as Buckinghamshire Battalion. Both the University and Eton College became part of the newly created Officers Training Corps.

40. Other ranks' helmet plate, 2nd Oxfordshire Rifle Volunteer Corps.

ESSEX REGIMENT

The several regiments comprising Number 34 Sub-District Brigade formed the Essex Regiment in 1881 — 1st Battalion (late 44th Foot), 2nd Battalion (late 56th Foot), 3rd Battalion (late Essex Rifles Militia) and 4th Battalion (late West Essex Militia). The volunteers were provided by the 1st to 4th Essex Corps and these assumed the title of the Regiment in 1883.

1st Volunteer Battalion. "SOUTH AFRICA 1900-02"
The 3rd Essex Administrative Battalion of Rifle Volunteers included corps dating from 1859 and formed in the South of the County. Consolidated as 1st Corps in 1880, the Battalion at first comprised eight companies — Romford (2), Ilford, Barking, Walthamstow, Brentwood, Chipping Ongar and Hornchurch. Headquarters were moved from Ilford to Brentwood in 1890.

Additions to the Battalion were, two companies in 1896 followed by four more in 1900/01. One of these, however, had ceased to exist by 1902.

41. Sergeant-Major Baker, 4th Volunteer Battalion, Essex Regiment.

2nd Volunteer Battalion. "SOUTH AFRICA 1900-02"
This battalion dates from 1859 and was previously the 2nd Essex Rifle Volunteer Corps and before that the County's 1st Administrative Battalion. Upon consolidation in 1880 there were eight companies located — Chelmsford (2), Colchester (2), Witham, Braintree, Maldon and Walton on the Naze. Battalion Headquarters moved from Braintree to Colchester in 1895 and two additional companies were formed in 1900.

3rd Volunteer Battalion. "SOUTH AFRICA 1900-02"
The 5th Essex Rifle Volunteer Corps was formed at Plaistow in 1859 and renumbered as 3rd in 1880. Headquarters moved from Plaistow to West Ham in 1885 and the Battalion's original eight company establishment was increased to thirteen in 1900.

4th Volunteer Battalion. "SOUTH AFRICA 1900-02"
The 4th Volunteer Battalion was formed as the 9th Essex Rifle Volunteer Corps at Silvertown in 1860. Renumbered as 4th Corps in 1880, the Battalion had six companies — Hackney (4), Stratford and Silvertown, adding one more at Silvertown in 1892. Extra volunteers due to the war in South Africa provided the battalion with another four companies in 1900. Headquarters moved to Leyton in 1900.

Uniform
All four battalions originally wore green uniforms, the 1st having black facings. In 1895 permission to adopt scarlet with white facings was received by the 3rd and in 1902 the 4th also assumed the uniform of the Essex Regiment.

Territorial Force
The 1st to 4th Volunteer Battalions provided the Regiment's 4th to 7th Battalions (TF) in 1908.

SHERWOOD FORESTERS (NOTTINGHAMSHIRE AND DERBYSHIRE REGIMENT)

In 1881 the several regiments connected with the Counties of Nottinghamshire and Derbyshire were organised to form the Sherwood Foresters (Derbyshire Regiment). It was not until 1902, however, that Nottinghamshire was included in the title of the Regiment. The Foresters comprised — 1st Battalion (late 45th Foot), 2nd Battalion (late 95th Foot), 3rd Battalion (late 2nd Derbyshire Militia), 4th Battalion (late Royal

42. Derbyshire Volunteers for South Africa on board the S.S. Avondale Castle, Southampton 23rd February, 1900.

Sherwood Foresters Militia) and 5th Battalion (late 1st Derbyshire Militia). The volunteers, two corps from each county, were, save for the 1st Nottinghamshire, designated as volunteer battalions in 1887.

1st Volunteer Battalion. "SOUTH AFRICA 1900-02"

The senior company of the Battalion was formed in 1859 and was included in the 1st Administrative Battalion of Derbyshire Rifle Volunteers from 1860. The 1st Admin. was consolidated as 1st Corps in 1880; its headquarters being in Derby and an establishment of twelve companies located — Derby (7), Butterley, Condor Park, Belper and Long Eaton (2).

2nd Volunteer Battalion. "SOUTH AFRICA 1900-02"

When the 3rd Administrative Battalion of Derbyshire Rifle Volunteers was consolidated in 1880 it at first took on the number of its senior corps — the 3rd (formed in 1860). This was soon changed to 2nd, the new battalion's headquarters being placed in Bakewell and its ten company establishment being located — Chesterfield, Chapel-en-le-Frith, Ashbourne, Bakewell, Wirksworth, Matlock, Clay Cross, Whaley Bridge, Hartington and Staveley.

Battalion headquarters moved to Chesterfield in 1898 and in 1900 an increase in volunteers brought about the formation of three new companies at Chesterfield (2) and Buxton.

1st Nottinghamshire (Robin Hood) Volunteer Rifle Corps. "SOUTH AFRICA 1900-02"

Although ranked as 3rd Volunteer Battalion, the 1st Nottinghamshire Rifle Volunteer Corps did not assume the title of the Regiment. Formed in 1859, the "Robin Hoods" were from Nottingham, where by 1881 an establishment of ten companies was maintained. The strength of the Battalion was increased by one company in 1895, and then by another in the following year. Finally, and as a result of the increase in volunteers due to the war in South Africa, six more companies were sanctioned during 1900/01. Now with eighteen companies, including two comprising cyclists, the 1st Nottinghamshire was divided into two battalion.

4th (Nottinghamshire) Volunteer Battalion. "SOUTH AFRICA 1900-02"

The Nottinghamshire corps outside Nottingham were, in 1860, organised into the County's 1st Administrative Battalion. Twenty years later the Battalion was consolidated as 2nd Corps, its headquarters at that time being in East Retford and its eight companies located — East Retford, Newark (2), Mansfield, Thorney Wood Chase, Collingham, Worksop and Southwell. Headquarters were moved to Newark in 1890.

Uniform
Both the 1st and 2nd Volunteer Battalions wore scarlet uniforms with white facings, the later changing from blue facings around 1886. In Nottinghamshire, the Robin Hoods had green with black facings, the Army List specifying Lincoln green from 1893, while the 4th Volunteer Battalion wore scarlet and Lincoln green facings.

Territorial Force
The four volunteer battalions provided the Regiment's four Territorial Force battalions (5th – 8th) in order of seniority.

LOYAL NORTH LANCASHIRE REGIMENT

The Loyal North Lancashire Regiment was formed out of the several units comprising Number 12 Sub-District — 1st Battalion (late 47th Foot), 2nd Battalion (late 81st Foot) 3rd and 4th Battalions (late 3rd Royal Lancashire Militia) and the 11th and 14th Lancashire Rifle Volunteer Corps.

1st Volunteer Battalion. "SOUTH AFRICA 1900-02"
The 11th Lancashire Rifle Volunteer Corps was formed at Preston in 1859 and with other corps from Longton, Leyland and Chorley formed the 6th Administrative Battalion of Lancashire Rifle Volunteers. The 6th Admin. Battalion was consolidated as 11th Corps in 1880, and three years later this became the 1st Volunteer Battalion. The nine original companies of the Battalion were located — Preston (5), Leyland and Chorley (3), two new companies being sanctioned in 1900.

2nd Volunteer Battalion. "SOUTH AFRICA 1900-02"
The 2nd Volunteer Battalion was from Bolton, where the 27th Lancashire Rifle Volunteer Corps was formed in 1859. In 1876 the 27th was amalgamated with the 82nd Corps at Hindley. The number was changed to 14th in 1880, and then in 1883, the title — 2nd Volunteer Battalion was assumed. The original establishment was ten companies, an additional two being sanctioned in 1900.

Uniform
Both battalions wore scarlet tunics with white facings, the 2nd having green facings until 1883.

Territorial Force
In 1908 both battalions transferred to the Territorial Force, the 1st as the Regiment's 4th Battalion and the 2nd as the 5th.

43. Corporal-Bugler, 2nd Volunteer Battalion, Loyal North Lancashire Regiment.

44. 1st Volunteer Battalion, Northamptonshire Regiment. (John Woodroff)

NORTHAMPTONSHIRE REGIMENT

Both the Counties of Northamptonshire and Rutlandshire supplied the battalions that made up Number 29 Sub-District prior to 1881. In that year the Northamptonshire Regiment was formed and its battalions were organised — 1st (late 48th Foot), 2nd (late 58th Foot), 3rd and 4th Battalions (late Northamptonshire and Rutlandshire Militia) and the 1st Northamptonshire Rifle Volunteer Corps.

1st Volunteer Battalion. "SOUTH AFRICA 1900-02"
The County of Northamptonshire's rifle volunteers were organised into an administrative battalion in 1860. This in turn became the 1st Corps in 1880, and then in 1887, the 1st Volunteer Battalion, Northamptonshire Regiment.

Headquarters of the Battalion were at Northampton and its original thirteen companies located at — Althorpe, Towcester, Northampton (5), Peterborough (2), Wellingborough (2), Daventry and Kettering. One company was lost in 1885, but during the Boer War an additional four were sanctioned.

Uniform
The uniform of the Battalion was grey with scarlet facings.

Territorial Force
In 1908 the Battalion in the main transferred to the Territorial Force as the 4th Battalion, Northamptonshire Regiment (TF). However, a number of companies did provide a nucleus for artillery and other units.

PRINCESS CHARLOTTE OF WALES'S (ROYAL BERKSHIRE REGIMENT)

In 1881 the four battalions comprising Number 41 Sub-District were formed into the Princess Charlotte of Wales's (Berkshire Regiment), the Regiment being granted its "Royal" title in 1885. The 49th and 66th Regiments of Foot provided the 1st and 2nd Regular Battalions while the 3rd was made up from the old Royal Berkshire Militia. The 1st Berkshire Rifle Volunteer Corps provided the Regiment's volunteers and assumed the title of 1st Volunteer Battalion in 1882.

1st Volunteer Battalion. "SOUTH AFRICA 1900-02"
The several rifle volunteer corps in Berkshire were amalgamated in 1873 under the title of 1st Corps. The senior of the thirteen companies involved had been formed at Reading in 1859 and

together with all other Berkshire corps had comprised the County's 1st Admin. Battalion.

With headquarters and three companies at Reading, the remainder of the Battalion were originally located at — Windsor, Newbury, Abingdon, Maidenhead, Sandhurst, Faringdon, Wantage, Winkfield, Wallingford and Windsor Great Park. The cadets from Coopers Hill College later provided a company and another comprising 'Mounted Infantry' appeared in 1885/86.

Uniform
The battalion changed from grey to scarlet in 1879, the blue facings of the line battalions replacing the volunteers' Lincoln green in 1886.

Territorial Force
The Battalion formed the 4th Royal Berkshire Regiment (TF) in 1908.

45. 1st Volunteer Battalion, Princess Charlotte of Wales's (Royal Berkshire Regiment).

QUEEN'S OWN
(ROYAL WEST KENT REGIMENT)

The various regiments comprising Number 46 Sub-District Brigade formed the Queen's Own (Royal West Kent Regiment) in 1881 — 1st Battalion (late 50th Foot), 2nd Battalion (late 97th Foot), 3rd and 4th Battalions (late West Kent Militia). The original volunteer battalions were provided by the 1st, 3rd and 4th Kent Rifle Volunteer Corps, and these assumed the name of the Regiment in 1883.

1st Volunteer Battalion. "SOUTH AFRICA 1900-02"
The 2nd Administrative Battalion of Kent Rifle Volunteers (senior corps formed in 1859) was consolidated in 1877 to form the 1st Kent Rifle Volunteer Corps. At this time headquarters were placed at Tonbridge and an establishment of eight companies located — Maidstone (2), Tonbridge, Tunbridge Wells, Penshurst, Leeds Castle, Sevenoaks and Westerham. Three new companies, one of them a cyclist, were added to the Battalion in 1900.

2nd Volunteer Battalion. "SOUTH AFRICA 1900-02"
The 1st Kent Administrative Battalion, comprising corps all raised during 1859/60, was consolidated as 3rd Kent (West Kent) Rifle Volunteer Corps in 1880. Battalion headquarters was in Blackheath and an original establishment of eleven companies was located at — Lee (2), Dartford (2), Greenwich, Bromley, Blackheath (2), Deptford (2) and Charlton. With an additional two companies, one a cyclist, formed at Blackheath in 1900, the strength of the 2nd Volunteer Battalion in 1908 stood at thirteen companies.

3rd Volunteer Battalion. "SOUTH AFRICA 1901-02"
This battalion, comprising ten companies, was from Woolwich where the 4th Kent Rifle Volunteer Corps was formed in 1859. Also from Woolwich, and in particular, the Royal Arsenal, were the 21st and 26th Kent. These were merged in 1870 and then in 1880 joined the 4th under that title.

4th Volunteer Battalion. "SOUTH AFRICA 1902"
The 4th Volunteer Battalion was formed with an establishment of nine companies in 1900. Headquarters were at Chatham but the locations of only two companies — "G" and "H" at King Street, New Brompton, are known.

Uniform
The 1st, 3rd and 4th Volunteer Battalions had scarlet with blue facings, the 1st changing from all green in 1893 and the 3rd

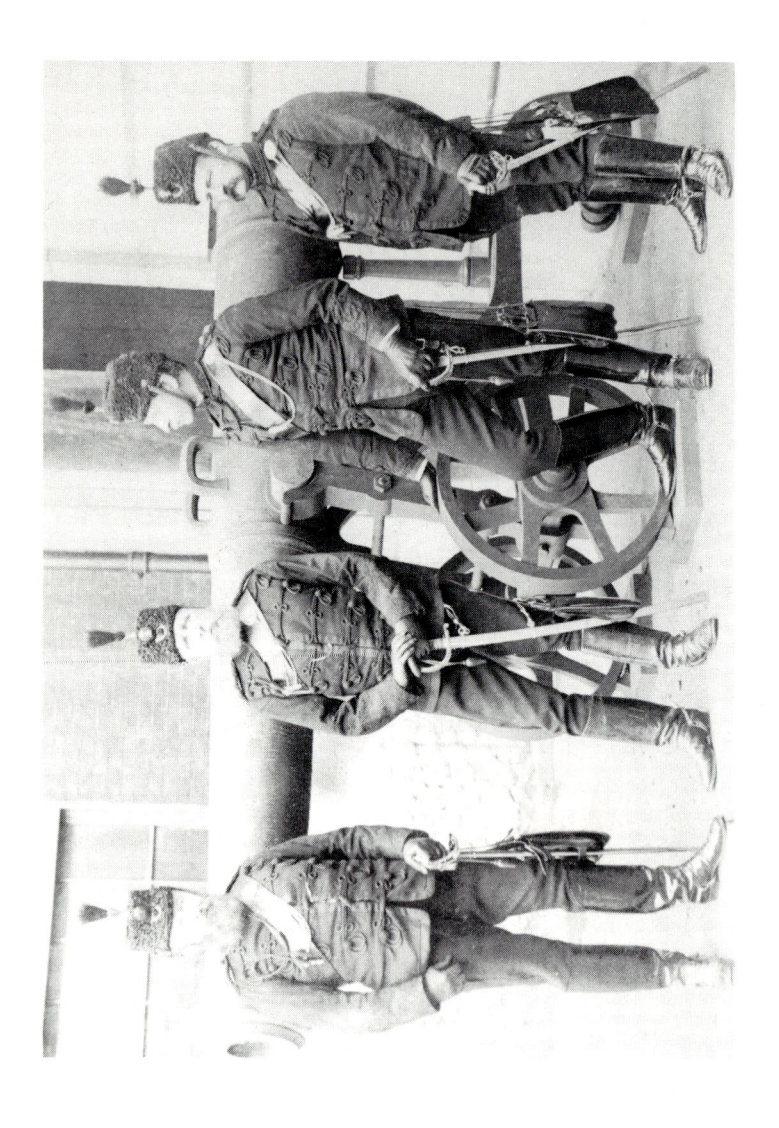

46. From left to right: Major William F. Despard, Lieut.-Colonel John D.C. Farrell (Commanding Officer), Captain Dacres C. Belgrave (Adjutant) and Major Charles D. Davies, 3rd Volunteer Battalion, Queen's Own (Royal West Kent Regiment) c1881. (Army Museums Ogilby Trust)

from green with scarlet facings, also in 1893. The 2nd Volunteer Battalion wore green with black facings.

Territorial Force
The 1st Volunteer Battalion provided personnel for both the 4th and 5th Battalions (TF) in 1908, while the 2nd and 3rd formed the 20th Battalion of the London Regiment. The 4th Volunteer Battalion was disbanded with effect from 31st March, 1908.

KING'S OWN
(YORKSHIRE LIGHT INFANTRY)

The several battalions comprising Number 8 Sub-District Brigade in 1881 formed the King's Own Light Infantry (South Yorkshire Regiment), title changed to the above in 1887. The 1st and 2nd Battalions were provided by the 51st and 105th Regiments of Foot respectively and the single militia battalion (3rd) was provided by the 1st West Yorks. There was one volunteer corps, the 5th Yorkshire (West Riding) and this received the title of the Regiment in 1883.

47. 1st Volunteer Battalion, King's Own (Yorkshire Light Infantry) 1904. (B. Nevison)

1st Volunteer Battalion. "SOUTH AFRICA 1900-02"
The West Riding of Yorkshire formed its 3rd Administrative Battalion of Rifle Volunteers in 1860, its headquarters being placed at Wakefield the home of its senior corps (formed in 1859). In 1880 the Battalion was consolidated as 5th Yorkshire (West Riding) Rifle Volunteer Corps, its establishment then being ten companies located — Wakefield (4), Goole, Dewsbury (3), Batley (2). This number was maintained up till 1908, locations however by this time being — Wakefield (3), Dewsbury (2), Batley (2), Normanton, Goole and Ossett.

Uniform
The Battalion wore scarlet jackets with blue facings.

Territorial Force
The Battalion provided personnel for both the 4th and 5th Battalions (TF).

KING'S (SHROPSHIRE LIGHT INFANTRY)

The King's Light Infantry (Shropshire Regiment) (title changed in 1882) was formed in 1881 from the 53rd Foot (1st Battalion), 85th Foot (2nd Battalion), Shropshire Militia (3rd Battalion), Herefordshire Militia (4th Battalion) and the Rifle Volunteers of Shropshire and Herefordshire (3 corps).

1st Volunteer Battalion. "SOUTH AFRICA 1900-02"
The 1st Shropshire Rifle Volunteer Corps was formed at Shrewsbury in 1859 and in the following year was united with other corps as the 1st Administrative Battalion of Shropshire Rifle Volunteers. In 1880 this battalion was consolidated as 1st Corps, headquarters being in Shrewsbury and its eight companies located at — Shrewsbury (2), Condover, Ironbridge, Shifnal, Bridgnorth, Ludlow and Cleobury Mortimer. Redesignation as 1st Volunteer Battalion was in 1887.

2nd Volunteer Battalion. "SOUTH AFRICA 1900-02"
Also raised in 1859 was the 2nd Shropshire Rifle Volunteer Corps, and like the 1st, formed part of an administrative battalion with other Shropshire corps. In 1880 this battalion was consolidated as 2nd Corps; the title of 2nd Volunteer Battalion following in 1887.
 The 2nd Corps, which moved its headquarters from Shrewsbury to Newport shortly after consolidation, at first had seven companies — Market Drayton, Whitchurch,

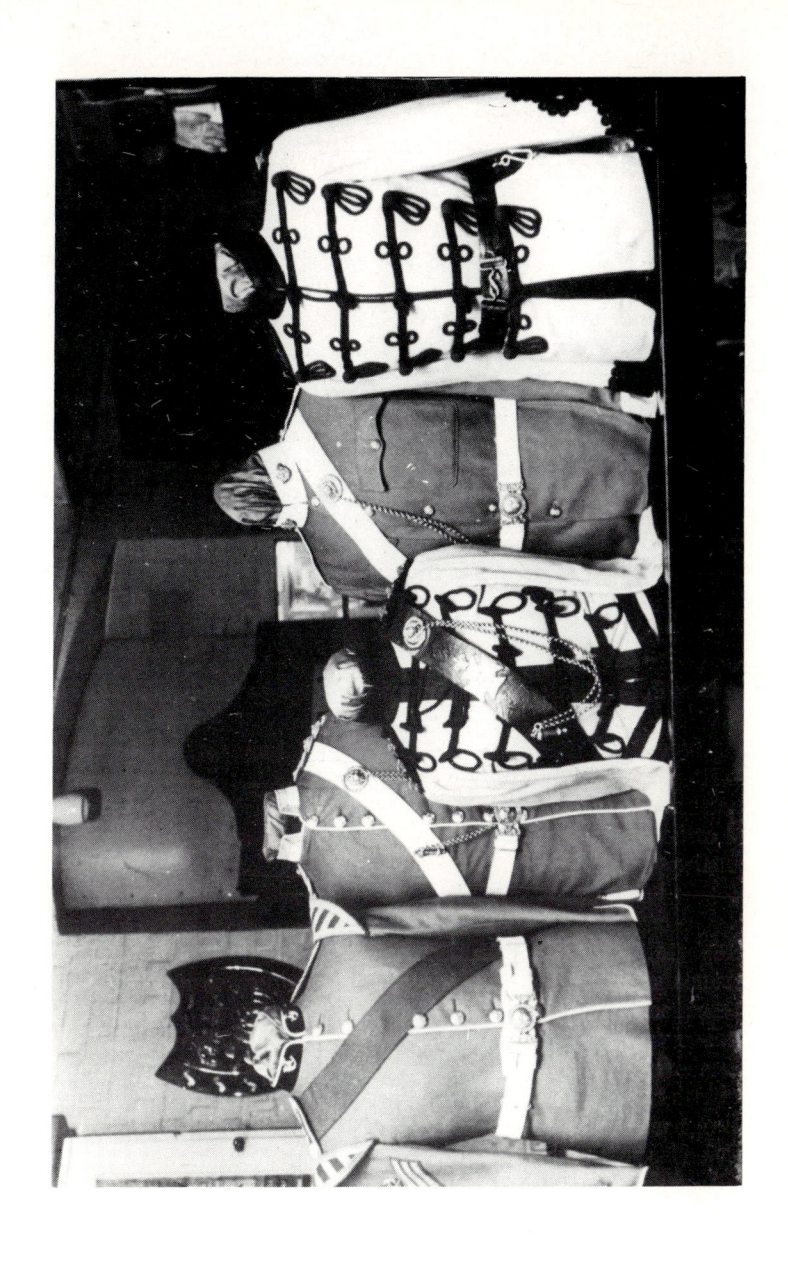

48. Uniforms of 1st and 2nd Volunteer Battalions, Kings (Shropshire Light Infantry). (G. Archer Parfitt)

Wellington, Hodnet, Wem, Oswestry and Newport. In 1885 an old corps, disbanded in 1879, was revived at Dllesmere, and this was added to the Battalion as 'H' Company.

1st Herefordshire Volunteer Rifle Corps.
"SOUTH AFRICA 1900-02"

Although ranked as 3rd Volunteer Battalion, the 1st Herefordshire Volunteer Rifle Corps did not assume the title of its regiment. Originating in 1860 the several rifle volunteer companies of Herefordshire were in 1864 united with those from the neighbouring County of Radnorshire. In 1880 these companies were merged as 1st Herefordshire Rifle Volunteer Corps, headquarters being situated in Hereford with ten companies located — Hereford (2), Ross (2), Ledbury, Bromyard, Leominster, Kington, Presteigne and Rhayader. There was also a half company at Hereford.

In 1881 'E' Company was merged with 'B' at Ross. A new 'E' Company was formed at Weobley in 1889 and that same year a Bearer Company was formed at Hereford to serve the Welsh Border Infantry Brigade, although this was borne as part of the strength of 'A' Company. Several other changes in organisation took place in 1905. 'L' Company was formed at Hereford from members of the Cyclist Section created there in 1888, and 'M' was also formed at Ruardean. An amalgamation between 'I' and 'G' Companies reduced the strength of the battalion and the Bearer Company became a separate unit designated as the Welsh Border Brigade Company RAMC (V).

Uniform

The 1st Volunteer Battalion wore scarlet uniforms with white facings until 1898, when blue collars and cuffs were adopted. In the 2nd Volunteer Battalion, Grey with black facings were worn throughout its history, while in Herefordshire these same colours were changed for scarlet and black in 1875.

Territorial Force

In 1908 both the Shropshire battalions were merged to form the Regiment's 4th Battalion (TF). At the same time the Herefordshire Volunteers were at first allotted the title — Herefordshire Battalion, The King's (Shropshire Light Infantry), but after a few months this was changed to — The Herefordshire Regiment.

49. Sergeant-Major George Means, 17th Middlesex (North Middlesex) Volunteer Rifle Corps c1896.

DUKE OF CAMBRIDGE'S OWN (MIDDLESEX REGIMENT)

This regiment was formed out of Number 50 Sub-District Brigade — 1st Battalion (late 57th Foot), 2nd Battalion (late 77th Foot), 3rd Battalion (late Royal Elthorne Militia) and 4th Battalion (late Royal East Middlesex Militia). The volunteers were provided by the 3rd, 8th and 17th Middlesex Corps.

1st Volunteer Battalion. "SOUTH AFRICA 1900-02"

In 1880 the 2nd Administrative Battalion of Middlesex Rifle Volunteers (senior company formed in 1859) was consolidated as the County's 3rd Corps. At this time headquarters were placed in Hornsey and the Battalion's original nine companies were located at — Hampstead (2), Barnet, Hornsey, Highgate (2), Tottenham and Enfield (2). A tenth company was formed at Enfield in 1881 and the title — 1st Volunteer Battalion was assumed in 1898.

With an increase in volunteers due to the war in South Africa, the Battalion, in 1900, was given permission to increase its establishment by three companies. This was carried out and at the end of 1900 company locations were — Hampstead, Barnet, Hornsey (4), Highgate (2), Tottenham (3) and Enfield (2).

By 1905 it was realised that recruits were not coming forward in sufficient numbers to maintain a thirteen company establishment. Subsequently permission to reduce this to nine was received, and from 1905 locations were — Hampstead, Barnet, Hornsey (3), Highgate, Tottenham and Enfield (2).

2nd Volunteer Battalion. "SOUTH AFRICA 1900-02"

The 7th Administrative Battalion of Middlesex Rifle Volunteers (senior company raised in 1860) was consolidated as the 8th Middlesex (South West Middlesex) Rifle Volunteer Corps in 1880, and in 1887 redesignated as 2nd Volunteer Battalion. With headquarters in Hounslow, the Battalion's original eight companies were located — Hounslow (4), Uxbridge, Ealing, Sunbury and Staines. In 1900 an increase in establishment by two companies was authorised. However, four years later this was reduced again to eight.

11th Middlesex (Railway) Rifle Volunteer Corps.

The 11th Middlesex joined the Regiment from the King's Royal Rifle Corps in 1882. It transferred to the Royal Fusiliers in 1890.

17th Middlesex (North Middlesex) Volunteer Rifle Corps. "SOUTH AFRICA 1900-02"

Formed in 1860 as the 29th Middlesex Rifle Volunteer Corps and renumbered in 1880 as 17th, the Battalion maintained eight companies at its headquarters in High Street, Camden Town.

Uniform

The 1st Volunteer Battalion wore grey uniforms until 1898 when the scarlet and white facings of the Middlesex Regiment were adopted. Lemon yellow facings replaced the white in 1902. Grey was also worn by the 2nd Volunteer Battalion, scarlet and white being introduced by 1896. In the 17th Middlesex, an all green uniform was taken into use in 1904, black facings being worn prior to that.

Territorial Force

In 1908 the 1st and 2nd Volunteer Battalions formed the Regiment's 7th and 8th Battalions (TF) respectively. The 17th Middlesex became the 19th Battalion of the London Regiment.

KING'S ROYAL RIFLE CORPS

The King's Royal Rifle Corps in 1881, comprised four line battalions (late 60th Foot), five Militia battalions provided by the Huntingdon, Royal Flint, Royal 2nd Middlesex, Carlow and North Cork Regiments, and a number of volunteer battalions from the Metropolitan area.

1st Middlesex (Victoria and St. George's) Volunteer Rifle Corps. "SOUTH AFRICA 1900-02"

Sanction to form a volunteer corps, known as the Victoria Volunteer Rifle Corps, was given in 1853. This later became the 1st Middlesex, which in 1881, together with the 6th Middlesex, formed a volunteer battalion of the King's Royal Rifle Corps. In 1892 the two corps were amalgamated. At that time the 1st Corps was located at St John's Wood in North West London, while the 6th, in Davies Street Westminster, provided headquarters for the new corps. Upon amalgamation the establishment of the Battalion was set at eight companies. This, however, was increased to ten during the Boer War.

2nd Middlesex (South Middlesex) Volunteer Rifle Corps. "SOUTH AFRICA 1900-02"

This battalion was formed in 1859 at Walham Green, London. It moved to Putney Bridge in 1902 and maintained an establishment of twelve companies.

4th Middlesex (Kensington) Volunteer Rifle Corps.
"SOUTH AFRICA 1900-02"
The 4th Middlesex Rifle Volunteer Corps was formed in 1859 and moved its headquarters from the West End of London to Kensington in 1885. The strength of the Battalion was seven, and from 1886, eight companies.

5th Middlesex (West Middlesex) Volunteer Rifle Corps.
"SOUTH AFRICA 1900-02"
Formed in 1859 as the 9th Middlesex Rifle Volunteer Corps (renumbered in 1880), the Battalion served as a volunteer battalion (six companies) of the Royal Fusiliers until 1883. With headquarters in St John's Wood, the corps merged with the 9th Middlesex (four companies) in 1899. It reached a strength of thirteen companies in 1901 but was reduced to twelve in 1904.

6th Middlesex (St George's) Volunteer Rifle Corps.
Formed in 1860 as the 11th Middlesex and renumbered 6th (six companies) in 1880. With the 1st Corps attached, the 6th provided a volunteer battalion from 1881. In 1892 the 1st and 6th were amalgamated as 1st Middlesex (Victoria and St George's). See 1st Middlesex above.

9th Middlesex Volunteer Rifle Corps.
Formed at Harrow in 1859 as 18th Corps. Renumbered 9th in 1880, the Corps served as part of the Royal Fusiliers until 1883. That year it transferred to the King's Royal Rifle Corps and together with the 5th Middlesex formed a volunteer battalion. Finally, in 1899, the 9th (four companies) was amalgamated with the 5th.

10th Middlesex Volunteer Rifle Corps.
Served as a volunteer battalion until transferring to the Royal Fusiliers in 1883.

11th Middlesex (Railway) Volunteer Rifle Corps.
Joined the Regiment as a volunteer battalion in 1881 but transferred to the Middlesex Regiment the following year.

The Prince of Wales's Own, 12th Middlesex (Civil Service) Volunteer Rifle Corps.
"SOUTH AFRICA 1900-02"
In 1860 a number of corps that had been formed by various Government departments in London were merged under the title of — 21st Middlesex (Civil Service) Rifle Volunteer Corps. Headquarters were placed at Somerset House and the original establishment of eight companies rose to ten in 1900. Having been renumbered in 1880, the 12th Middlesex received the title

50. Member of "I" (Cyclist) Company, The Prince of Wales's Own, 12th Middlesex (Civil Service) Volunteer Rifle Corps. (Army Museums Ogilby Trust)

"Prince of Wales's Own" in 1898, His Royal Highness having been Hon. Colonel of the Corps since its formation.

13th Middlesex (Queen's) Volunteer Rifle Corps. "SOUTH AFRICA 1900-02"

The Queen's Westminsters was formed in 1860 and designated as the 22nd Middlesex Rifle Volunteer Corps. Renumbered as 13th in 1880, the Corps maintained twelve companies, increasing to sixteen in 1900.

21st Middlesex (The Finsbury Rifle Volunteer Corps) Volunteer Rifle Corps. "SOUTH AFRICA 1900-02"

The Finsbury Rifles was formed as 39th Middlesex in 1860. It became 21st Corps in 1880 and from 1881 to 1883 served as a volunteer battalion of the Rifle Brigade. The Battalion maintained an establishment of ten companies raising to twelve in 1900.

22nd Middlesex (Central London Rangers). "SOUTH AFRICA 1900-02"

Formed in 1860, at Gray's Inn, as 40th Middlesex Rifle Volunteer Corps and renumbered 22nd in 1880. The Corps served as a volunteer battalion of the Royal Fusiliers from 1881 to 1882 and maintained an establishment of eight companies.

25th Middlesex (Bank of England) Volunteer Rifle Corps.

Formed as 50th Middlesex Rifle Volunteer Corps in 1875 and renumbered as 25th in 1880, the Corps had a strength of one company and was attached to the 12th Corps. It served with the 12th as a volunteer battalion until disbandment in April 1907.

26th Middlesex (Cyclist) Volunteer Rifle Corps.

The 26th Middlesex was formed in 1888 and bears the distinction of being the first and only volunteer corps completely dedicated to a cyclist role. With three companies, the Corps, together with the 2nd Middlesex formed a volunteer battalion of the King's Royal Rifle Corps. In the Army List, however, it appears under the Rifle Brigade. The 26th used a number of premises in the London area as headquarters. The last being at 45a Horseferry Road, Westminster.

27th Middlesex (Harrow School) Volunteer Rifle Corps.

This corps was formed out of the Harrow School Cadet Corps in April 1902 and maintained three companies until disbandment in January 1906.

1st London (City of London Rifle Volunteer Brigade) Volunteer Rifle Corps.
"SOUTH AFRICA 1900-02"
Formed in 1859, the Corps maintained an establishment of between ten and thirteen companies. Headquarters from 1893 were at 130 Bunhill Row E.C.

2nd London Volunteer Rifle Corps.
This corps was formed in 1860 from members of the newspaper and printing trade. Known unofficially as the "Printer's Battalion", the 2nd London had its last headquarters at 7a Farringdon Road, E.C. and maintained an establishment of ten companies.

3rd London (City of) Volunteer Rifle Corps.
"SOUTH AFRICA 1900-02"
Formed in 1861, the 3rd London maintained twelve companies.

4th London Volunteer Rifle Corps.
Formed in 1900, the 4th London comprised two companies, its members all having been educated at the Grocers' Company's Schools in Clapton, North East London. The 4th was attached to the 1st London and was disbanded in 1905.

Uniform
Uniform and facings colours were — 1st Middx: green/black later green/scarlet (the change indicated in the Army List in 1892). 2nd Middx: grey/scarlet, 4th Middx: grey/scarlet, 5th Middx: grey/scarlet later green/scarlet (the change indicated in the Army List in 1891), 6th Middx: green/black later green/scarlet (the change indicated in the Army List in 1886), 9th Middx: green, 12th Middx: dark grey/blue changing to light grey/blue in 1889, 13th Middx: grey/scarlet, 21st Middx: green/scarlet, 22nd Middx: green/scarlet, 25th Middx: green, 26th Middx: grey/scarlet, 27th Middx: neutral tint/dark blue, 1st London: dark green, 2nd London: green/scarlet, 3rd London: scarlet/buff, 4th London: green/scarlet.

Territorial Force
In 1908 the 2nd Middlesex provided much of the personnel for the 10th Battalion Middlesex Regiment while the 5th became that regiment's 9th Battalion. The remaining corps all provided battalions of the London Regiment — 1st Middx: (part of 9th Bn.), 4th Middx: (13th Bn.), 12th Middx: (15th Bn.), 13th Middx: (16th Bn.), 21st Middx:(11th Bn.), 22nd Middx: (12th Bn.), 26th Middx: (25th Bn.), 1st London: (5th Bn.), 2nd London: (6th Bn.), and 3rd London: (7th Bn.).

DUKE OF EDINBURGH'S (WILTSHIRE REGIMENT)

Formed out of the units comprising Number 38 Sub-District, the Regiment comprised — 1st Battalion (late 62nd Foot), 2nd Battalion (late 99th Foot), 3rd Battalion (late Royal Wiltshire Militia) and the 1st and 2nd Wiltshire Rifle Volunteer Corps.

1st Wiltshire Volunteer Rifle Corps.
"SOUTH AFRICA 1900-01"
The 1st Wiltshire Volunteer Rifle Corps, originating in 1859 and previously its County's 1st Administrative Battalion, served as the Regiment's 1st Volunteer Battalion. However, no change in title was ever assumed. With headquarters in Warminster the Battalion's eight companies in 1880 were located — Salisbury (2), Trowbridge (2), Bradford-on-Avon, Warminster, Westbury and Wilton. A new company was sanctioned at Tisbury in 1892 and in 1900 a company of cyclists at Bradford-on-Avon was also formed.

2nd Volunteer Battalion. "SOUTH AFRICA 1900-02"
Ten Wiltshire Rifle Corps comprising twelve companies were formed into the County's 2nd Admin. Battalion in 1861. In 1880 these were merged as 2nd Corps, and then in 1887 the title — 2nd Volunteer Battalion was assumed.

With headquarters at Chippenham the original companies of the 2nd were located at Malmesbury, Chippenham, Devizes (2), Market Lavington, Swindon (3), Melksham, Wootton Bassett, Marlborough and Highworth. A reduction was made to eleven companies in 1882 and then to ten in 1901.

Uniform
Both battalions wore green uniforms with black facings.

Territorial Force
In 1908 both battalions were merged to form the 4th Battalion, Wiltshire Regiment (TF).

51. 2nd Volunteer Battalion, Wiltshire Regiment Ambulance Waggon.

MANCHESTER REGIMENT

The Manchester Regiment was formed out of the several battalions comprising Number 16 Sub-District Brigade — 1st Battalion (late 63rd Foot), 2nd Battalion (late 96th Foot) and 3rd and 4th Battalions (late 6th Royal Lancashire Militia). The original volunteers, which received their volunteer battalion designations in 1888, were — 4th, 6th, 7th, 16th, 17th and 20th Lancashire Corps.

1st Volunteer Battalion. "SOUTH AFRICA 1900-02"
In 1880 the 4th Administrative Battalion of Lancashire Rifle Volunteers, comprising rifle corps from the eastern side of the County and dating from 1859, was consolidated as the 4th Lancashire Rifle Volunteer Corps. At this time headquarters were in Manchester and an establishment of thirteen companies was located — Wigan (5), Swinton, Eccles, Leigh, Atherton, Worsley, Farnworth (2) and Flixton. An additional company was formed in 1901.

2nd Volunteer Battalion. "SOUTH AFRICA 1900-02"
Formed in 1859, the 6th Lancashire Rifle Volunteer Corps was also known as the 1st Manchester. With headquarters in Stretford Road, Hulme, the Battalion's establishment in 1881 was twelve companies. One more was sanctioned in 1890, followed by another two, raised as a result of the extra volunteers who came forward during the war in South Africa.

3rd Volunteer Battalion. "SOUTH AFRICA 1900-02"
During 1859-60 a number of rifle volunteer companies were raised throughout Ashton-under-Lyne and Oldham. Two corps were formed — 23rd and 31st, and in 1880 these were amalgamated as the 7th Lancashire of twelve companies — Ashton (6), Oldham (6). In 1882 the establishment of the 7th Corps was reduced when the Oldham companies were removed to form a new corps designated as 22nd (later 6th Volunteer Battalion). Three additional companies were formed in 1900-01 and this remained the establishment of the 3rd Volunteer Battalion up to 1908.

4th Volunteer Battalion. "SOUTH AFRICA 1900-02"
The 4th Volunteer Battalion was formed in 1860 as the 40th Lancashire (3rd Manchester) Rifle Volunteer Corps. It was renumbered as 16th in 1880 and had its headquarters in Burlington Street, Manchester. In 1881 the Battalion's establishment stood at twelve companies. This was raised to thirteen in 1891.

52. The Earl of Crawford and Balcarres, Lieut.-Colonel 1st Volunteer Battalion, Manchester Regiment. (Wigan Metropolitan Borough Council)

17th Lancashire Rifle Volunteer Corps.
The 17th Corps, eight companies at Salford, joined the Manchester Regiment as one of its allotted volunteer battalions in 1881. It was transferred to the Lancashire Fusiliers in 1886.

5th (Ardwick) Volunteer Battalion. "SOUTH AFRICA 1900-02"
This battalion was originally the 33rd Lancashire (2nd Manchester) which was formed at Ardwick in 1860. Renumbered as 20th in 1880, the Corps originally comprised twelve companies, one more being added in 1900.

6th Volunteer Battalion. "SOUTH AFRICA 1901-02"
As mentioned in the 3rd Volunteer Battalion section, its six Oldham companies, formerly 31st Lancashire Rifle Volunteer Corps, were withdrawn in 1882 to form the County's 22nd Corps. By the end of 1882 the establishment had risen to eight companies and during the War in South Africa the formation of an additional two was sanctioned.

Uniform
The following details and changes of uniform are indicated in the Army List — 1st Volunteer Battalion: green with scarlet facings, 2nd: scarlet with yellow facings, 3rd: scarlet with green facings changing to white in 1885, 4th: scarlet with Lincoln green facings changing to white in 1888, 5th: green with scarlet facings, 6th: scarlet with Lincoln green facings changing to white in 1890.

Territorial Force
In 1908 the 1st to 6th Volunteer Battalions transferred to the Territorial Force as the Manchester Regiment's 5th, 6th, 9th, 7th, 8th and 10th Battalions respectively.

PRINCE OF WALES'S (NORTH STAFFORDSHIRE REGIMENT)

The North Staffordshire Regiment was formed in 1881 out of the units then comprising Number 20 Sub-District Brigade — 1st Battalion (late 64th Foot), 2nd Battalion (late 98th Foot), 3rd Battalion (late 2nd King's Own Stafford Militia), 4th Battalion (late 3rd King's Own Stafford Militia) and the 1st, 3rd and 4th Staffordshire Rifle Volunteer Corps. Under General Order 142 of June, 1882, the three volunteer corps were exchanged for those then forming part of the South Staffordshire Regiment — 2nd and 5th Staffordshire Corps. These battalions assumed the title of the Regiment in 1883.

53. Sergeant (stretcher bearer) 1st Volunteer Battalion, North Staffordshire Regiment. (Chris Coogan)

1st Volunteer Battalion. "SOUTH AFRICA 1900-02"
The 2nd Staffordshire (Staffordshire Rangers) Rifle Volunteer Corps was formed in 1880 by the consolidation of the County's 1st Administrative Battalion. At this time headquarters were at Stoke-upon-Trent and corps, located at Longton, Hanley, Burslem, Tunstall, Stoke-upon-Trent, Kidsgrove, Newcastle-under-Lyne, Leek, Hanley and Stone provided twelve companies. In 1900 three new companies were sanctioned — Eccleshall, Hanley, Buddulph. Later, however, the establishment was reduced to fourteen in 1902 and to thirteen in 1904.

2nd Volunteer Battalion. "SOUTH AFRICA 1900-02"
The 2nd Administrative Battalion of Staffordshire Rifle Volunteers was consolidated to form the County's 7th, later, 5th Corps in 1880. At this time, headquarters were situated at Lichfield and an eight company establishment was located at — Burton-on-Trent (3), Tamworth, Rugeley, Lichfield and Stafford (2). In 1884 battalion headquarters were moved to Burton-on-Trent and in 1900 a new company was formed at Uttoxeter.

Uniform
Both battalions wore scarlet uniforms with black facings, the 1st, however, changing to white facings by 1886.

Territorial Force
The Regiment's 5th and 6th Battalions (TF) were formed in order of seniority by the 1st and 2nd Volunteer Battalions.

YORK AND LANCASTER REGIMENT

The York and Lancaster Regiment was formed out of the units comprising Number 7 Sub-District — 1st Battalion (late 65th Foot), 2nd Battalion (late 84th Foot), 3rd Battalion (late 3rd West Yorkshire Militia) and the 2nd and 8th Yorkshire West Riding Rifle Volunteer Corps.

**1st (Hallamshire) Volunteer Battalion.
"SOUTH AFRICA 1900-02"**
Formed in Sheffield in 1859, the 2nd Yorkshire (West Riding) Corps was redesignated as 1st (Hallamshire) Volunteer Battalion, York and Lancaster Regiment in 1883. The establishment of the Battalion was raised from seven to eight companies in 1883 and then to nine in 1901.

2nd Volunteer Battalion. "SOUTH AFRICA 1900-02"

The 2nd Volunteer Battalion of the Regiment had its headquarters in Doncaster where the 4th Administrative Battalion of Yorkshire (West Riding) Rifle Volunteers was formed in 1860. When the Battalion was consolidated in 1880 the number assumed by the new corps was 18th, being that held at the time by its senior corps. However, within a few months this was changed to 8th, and then in 1883 the 2nd Volunteer Battalion title was assumed.

In 1880 the establishment of the 8th Corps was nine companies — Pontefract, Rotherham (3), Doncaster (2), Barnsley (2) and Wath-upon-Dearne. New companies were later added at Doncaster — one in 1884 and two in 1900.

Uniform
Scarlet tunics with white facings were worn by both battalions.

Territorial Force
In 1908 the 1st Volunteer Battalion provided the Regiment's 4th Battalion (TF) while the 2nd was split between the 5th and the 5th Battalion King's Own Yorkshire Light Infantry.

54. Other ranks' glengarry badge, 2nd Volunteer Battalion, York and Lancaster Regiment.

DURHAM LIGHT INFANTRY

The Durham Light Infantry was formed from the several regiments comprising Number 3 Sub-District Brigade — 1st Battalion (late 68th Foot), 2nd Battalion (late 106th Foot), 3rd Battalion (late 1st Durham Militia) and 4th Battalion (late 2nd Durham Militia). The volunteers were provided by the five Durham Corps which all assumed the title of the Regiment in 1887.

1st Volunteer Battalion. "SOUTH AFRICA 1900-02"
When the 4th Administrative Battalion (senior company formed in 1860) was consolidated as 1st Corps in 1880 it contained six companies in Durham — Stockton-on-Tees (3), Darlington (2), Castle Eden (1) and two in the North Yorkshire town of Middlesborough. four additional companies were raised — Stockton, Darlington, Middlesborough, Stockton (Cyclist), when an increase in volunteers occurred during the war in South Africa. Battalion Headquarters were in Stockton-on-Tees.

2nd Volunteer Battalion. "SOUTH AFRICA 1900-02"
The 2nd Administrative Battalion of Durham Rifle Volunteers was consolidated in 1880 as the County's 4th Corps. The original 4th had been formed in 1860 and was the senior element of the new corps. Within a few months, however, the Corps had been renumbered as 2nd. Its headquarters were placed at Bishop Auckland and the original establishment of six companies were located — Bishop Auckland, Coundon, Darlington, Middleton-in-Teesdale, Stanhope and Barnard Castle.

In 1883 the headquarters of "C" Company at Darlington was moved to Woodland. Three years later an additional two companies were sanctioned and subsequently raised at Spennymoor, but in 1899 the Middleton Company was closed down. Before the end of 1899, however, a replacement for Middleton had been established at Crook.

During the Boer War the Battalion's establishment was increased by three companies, one, a cyclist, being at Bishop Auckland and two at Consett. The last of the Battalion's company reorganisations took place in 1903 when "C" Company at Woodland moved to Shildon.

3rd (Sunderland) Volunteer Battalion. "SOUTH AFRICA 1900-02"
The 3rd Durham Rifle Volunteer Corps was formed at Sunderland in 1860 and by 1881 comprised six companies. A new company was sanctioned in 1900.

4th Volunteer Battalion. "SOUTH AFRICA 1900-02"
This battalion was formerly the County of Durham's 4th Corps and before that its 1st Administrative Battalion. Dating from 1860, the Battalion in 1881, comprised ten companies — Durham (3), Beamish, Chester-le-Street, Birtley, Washington and Felling (3).

Headquarters of the Battalion were moved from Chester-le-Street to Durham in 1890 and in 1892 "K" (Felling) Company was disbanded and its place taken by a new company formed at Stanley. In 1896 the remaining Felling Companies ("H" and "I") were amalgamated as "H", "I" being replaced by new personnel raised at Sacriston. The following year the headquarters of "H" company were moved from Felling to Houghton-le-Spring and at the same time the Felling personnel were withdrawn from the Battalion and transferred to the 5th Volunteer Battalion as its "L" Company. The last company of the Battalion was formed in 1900 when its cyclists were grouped together as "L" Company at Stanley.

5th Volunteer Battalion. "SOUTH AFRICA 1900-02"
The 5th Durham Rifle Volunteer Corps was formed in 1880 by the consolidation of the County's 3rd Administrative Battalion. Headquarters were placed at Gateshead and the Battalion's original eight companies were located at — Gateshead (3), South Shields (3), Blaydon Burn and Winlaton.

55. Officers' helmet 5th Volunteer Battalion, Durham Light Infantry.

By 1887 two companies — Gateshead and Winlaton, had been added to the establishment. This was followed by one at Felling in 1897 (see 4th V.B.) and a cyclist company at Blaydon in 1900.

Uniform
Three battalions wore scarlet — 1st (white facings), 3rd (blue facings changing to white in 1884) and 5th (green facings). Both the 2nd and 4th Volunteer Battalions had green uniforms with scarlet facings.

Territorial Force
The 1st to 5th Volunteer Battalions provided the Regiment's 5th to 9th Battalions (TF) in order of seniority.

HIGHLAND LIGHT INFANTRY

In 1881 the Highland Light Infantry comprised — 1st Battalion (late 71st Foot), 2nd Battalion (late 74th Foot), 3rd Battalion (late 1st Royal Lanark Militia) and the Lanarkshire Rifle Volunteer Corps numbered 5th, 6th, 8th, 9th and 10th. Of these, the 9th retained its title, while the remainder assumed volunteer battalion designations in 1887.

1st Volunteer Battalion. "SOUTH AFRICA 1900-02"
The 19th Lanarkshire Rifle Volunteer Corps was formed in Glasgow in 1859 and before the end of the following year had merged with other Glasgow companies under the title — 19th Lanarkshire (Glasgow 2nd Northern). In 1880 the Battalion was renumbered as 5th. An establishment of twelve companies was maintained through to 1908.

2nd Volunteer Battalion. "SOUTH AFRICA 1900-02"
This battalion originated in 1859/60 when a number of Clyde shipbuilding and engineering yards formed companies of rifle volunteers. In 1861 these companies were amalgamated under the title of 25th Lanarkshire Rifle Volunteer Corps and in 1880 this was changed to 6th. With headquarters in Yorkhill Street, Glasgow, the Battalion maintained eight companies until 1882, when an additional two were formed.

3rd (The Blythswood) Volunteer Battalion. "SOUTH AFRICA 1900-02"
On 10th May, 1865 the 2nd Administrative Battalion of Lanarkshire Rifle Volunteers was consolidated as the County's 31st Corps. At this time the Battalion included a number of independent companies which had been formed in Glasgow

56. Colour-sergeant, 3rd (The Blythswood) Volunteer Battalion, Highland Light Infantry post 1886. (Army Museums Ogilby Trust)

since 1859. The title "Blythswood Rifles" was added, as a compliment to the Battalion's commanding officer, Lieut.-Colonel Campbell of Blythswood, in June 1869. The Corps was renumbered as 8th in 1880 and maintained an establishment of twelve companies through to 1908.

9th Lanarkshire Volunteer Rifle Corps.
"SOUTH AFRICA 1900-02"
In 1880 the 3rd Administrative Battalion of Lanarkshire Rifle Volunteers (senior company formed in 1859) was consolidated as 9th Corps. At this time the Battalion comprised headquarters in Lanark and six companies — Lesmahagow, Lanark, Carluke, Douglas, Biggar and Leadhills. These six companies remained the establishment of the Battalion through to 1908, the Biggar Company transferring to Forth in 1894, and that at Leadhills to Law in 1901.

5th (Glasgow Highland) Volunteer Battalion.
"SOUTH AFRICA 1900-02"
In 1868 the 105th Lanarkshire (Glasgow Highland) Rifle Volunteer Corps, of twelve companies, was formed from Highlanders then resident in the City of Glasgow. Renumbered as 10th in 1880, the Battalion added a company of cyclists in 1900.

Uniform
1st Volunteer Battalion: Scarlet tunics with buff facings were worn till 1883, when doublets (yellow facings) and trews were adopted. Facings changed to buff in 1903. 2nd Volunteer Battalion: Scarlet tunics with black facings until 1904 when blue facings were introduced. In 1906, according to Records of the Scottish Volunteer Force by Lieut.-General Sir James Grierson, a complete change in uniform was sanctioned, the main features being, drab service doublets of H.L.I. pattern and Mackenzie tartan kilts. This was to be the sole dress of the Battalion, the officers, however, wore H.L.I. doublets and mess uniforms, with buff facings. 3rd Volunteer Battalion: Scarlet doublets with yellow facings and H.L.I. pattern trews replaced the Battalion's scarlet tunics and blue trousers and facings in 1886. 9th Lanarkshire: Scarlet tunics with blue facings were worn up till 1883 when doublets (yellow facings) and Mackenzie tartan trews were sanctioned. Facings were changed to buff in 1904. 5th Volunteer Battalion: The uniform of this battalion was styled on that for the Black Watch — scarlet doublets with blue facings and 42nd Tartan kilts.

Territorial Force
The Highland Light Infantry in 1908 was allotted five Territorial battalions (5th to 9th). These were formed by the Regiment's five volunteer battalions in order of senority.

57. Senior N.C.O.s (front) of the 1st (Ross Highland) Volunteer Battalion, Seaforth Highlanders July 1887. The N.C.O.s behind, and wearing feather bonnets, are from the 3rd (Militia) Battalion. (Queen's Own Highlanders Regimental Museum).

125

SEAFORTH HIGHLANDERS (ROSS-SHIRE BUFFS, THE DUKE OF ALBANY'S)

The Seaforth Highlanders in 1881, contained two line battalions (late 72nd and 78th Foot), the Highland Rifle Militia, which formed the 3rd Battalion, and four rifle volunteer corps.

1st Inverness-shire (Inverness Highland) Rifle Volunteer Corps.
This corps joined the Regiment in 1881 but was transferred to the Cameron Highlanders in 1883.

1st (Ross Highland) Volunteer Battalion.
"SOUTH AFRICA 1900-02"
The title assumed by the 1st Administrative Battalion of Ross-shire Rifle Volunteers in 1880 was — 1st Ross-shire (Ross Highland) Rifle Volunteer Corps. The Battalion had been formed in 1861 and contained the nine rifle corps that had been raised within the County since 1860. Headquarters were at Dingwall and the original companies located at — Tain, Dingwall, Fortrose, Munlochy, Ullapool, Invergordon, Evanton, Moy and Gairloch. The title — 1st (Ross Highland) Volunteer Battalion was assumed in 1887 and that same year the headquarters of the Evanton and Moy Companies were moved to Dingwall and Fairburn respectively.

1st Sutherland (The Sutherland Highland) Volunteer Rifle Corps.
"SOUTH AFRICA 1900-02"
This corps served as the Regiment's 2nd Volunteer Battalion, but that title was never assumed. The 1st Sutherland was created in 1880 by the consolidation of the 1st Administrative Battalion of Sutherland Rifle Volunteers. Not only that county contributed corps, but companies were also included from Caithness and the Orkneys and Shetlands, many dating from 1859/60.

Headquarters of the Battalion were at Golspie and its original ten companies located — Golspie, Dornoch, Brora, Rogart, Bonar Bridge, Lerwick, Thurso, Wick, Halkirk and Watten. In 1884 the Lerwick Company was disbanded and replaced by one at Lairg. Two additional companies were later sanctioned, one at Wick in 1890 followed by another at Reay in 1901.

3rd (Morayshire) Volunteer Battalion.
"SOUTH AFRICA 1900-02"
The 3rd Volunteer Battalion was from the County of Elgin and

had its origins in the several rifle volunteer corps that were formed there between 1860 and 1871. Formed into an administrative battalion at Elgin, and then in 1880 as one corps numbered 1st, the Battalion's original ten and a half companies were located at Forres (2), Elgin (2), Rothes, Fochabers, Abernethy, Urquhart, Garmouth and Grantown. The half company was at Pluscarden and was increased to a full company in 1897, its headquarters moving to Alves seven years later. Redesignation as 3rd (Morayshire) Volunteer Battalion took place in 1887 and in 1905 the Urquhart Company moved to Lhanbryde.

Uniform
In 1875 the Ross volunteers adopted a uniform that included scarlet doublets with blue facings and Mackenzie tartan trews. After 1880, kilts were gradually reintroduced into the Battalion, the uniform of the Seaforth Highlanders being authorized in 1888. The 1st Sutherland Rifle Volunteers wore scarlet with yellow facings and were permitted to retain their Sutherland pattern tartan. In the 3rd Volunteer Battalion scarlet tunics with blue facings were worn up to 1886 when authorisation was given for the adoption of scarlet doublets with yellow facings, and Mackenzie tartan trews. Kilts were authorised in 1898 and in 1905 the yellow facings became buff.

Territorial Force
In 1908 the three battalions formed in order of seniority, the 4th, 5th and 6th Seaforth Highlanders (TF).

GORDON HIGHLANDERS

In 1881 the Gordon Highlanders comprised two line battalions, formerly the 75th and 92nd Regiments, a militia battalion, late Royal Aberdeen Militia and six volunteer battalions provided by the Counties of Aberdeenshire, Kincardineshire and Banffshire. The volunteers assumed the title of the Regiment in 1884 and a seventh was later raised in Shetland.

1st Volunteer Battalion. "SOUTH AFRICA 1900-02"
The Battalion was formerly the 1st Aberdeenshire Rifle Volunteer Corps and was formed within the City in 1859. In 1881 the official establishment of the Battalion stood at eleven companies, however, at this time only eight existed and these were located — seven in Aberdeen and one just outside the City of Woodford.

An increase in strength by two companies came about in 1895. Three years later university students in Aberdeen formed a company, but this was to replace one that had just been broken up. The last change in establishment came in 1905 when four Aberdeen companies were amalgamated to form two.

2nd Volunteer Battalion. "SOUTH AFRICA 1900"
In 1880 the 2nd Administrative Battalion of Aberdeenshire Rifle Volunteers (senior company raised in 1859) was consolidated as the County's 2nd Corps. The strength of the Battalion at this time stood at seven companies — Methlie, Ellon, Newburgh, Turriff, Fyvie, Meldrum and Tarves, and this remained the organisation untill 1908. Battalion Headquarters moved from Aberdeen to Old Meldrum in 1899.

3rd (The Buchan) Volunteer Battalion. "SOUTH AFRICA 1900-01"
The 3rd Administrative Battalion of Aberdeenshire Rifle Volunteers was formed in 1862 from a number of corps that had been raised since 1859 in the area of north-east of Aberdeenshire known as "The Buchan". In 1880 the 3rd Admin. was consolidated as 3rd Corps with headquarters at Old Deer and nine companies located — New Deer, Peterhead, St Fergus, Old Deer, Strichen, Longside, Fraserburgh, New Pitsligo and Cruden.

Before 1908 numerous changes were made within the Battalion. Headquarters were moved to Peterhead in 1883 and in that same year those of "H" (New Pitsligo) Company transferred to Fraserburgh and a new company was raised at Boddam. In 1885 "C" (St Fergus) Company went to Crimond and in 1888 was again moved, this time to Lonmay. Also in 1888 the new company at Boddam ("K") was transferred to Peterhead. In 1900 the Cruden Company was disbanded and in the following year "C" Company was again involved when it was absorbed into "E" at Strichen.

4th (Donside Highland) Volunteer Battalion. "SOUTH AFRICA 1900-01"
This battalion was previously the 4th Aberdeenshire Rifle Volunteer Corps and before that the County's 1st Administrative Battalion. Companies dated from 1859, and in 1881 these were located at Huntly, Kildrummy, Insch, Alford, Inverurie, Kemnay and Auchmull. Battalion Headquarters were in Aberdeen and the title "Donside Highland" was added in February 1893.

In 1897 a new company was formed at Auchmull followed by two more — Kintore and Kildrummy in 1899. Other changes were in 1899, when the headquarters of "B" Company at Kildrummy moved to Strathdon, in 1903 when "G" and "H" (Auchmull) went to Bucksburn, and in 1906 when "B"

58. Captain W.E. Hutchison, 3rd (The Buchan) Volunteer Battalion, Gordon Highlanders. (Army Museums Ogilby Trust)

(Strathdon) and "C" (Insch) were amalgamated as "B" (Kildrummy).

5th (Deeside Highland) Volunteer Battalion.
"SOUTH AFRICA 1900-02"

In 1876 four Aberdeenshire rifle volunteer corps were transferred to the 1st Administrtive Battalion of Kincardineshire Rifle Volunteers, the Battalion at this time being under strength. The title assumed upon consolidation in 1880 was 1st Kincardineshire and Aberdeenshire (Deeside Highland) Rifle Volunteer Corps. Headquarters of the new corps were placed at Banchory and its establishment of ten companies located five in Kincardineshire — Banchory, Laurencekirk, Portlethen, Durris, Maryculter, and five in Aberdeenshire — Echt, Tarland, Aboyne, Ballater and Torphins.

A series of company mergers and changes in location began in November 1883 when the Torphins Company was absorbed into that at Banchory and its place taken by a new formation at Stonehaven. This was followed in May 1885 by the merger of "G" (Tarland) and "H" (Aboyne) Companies. Battalion Headquarters were moved to Aberdeen in the following year, and in 1887 and 1891 respectively "E" (Maryculter) Company transferred to Peterculter and "F" (Echt) went to Skene. Finally, in 1894, Battalion headquarters were moved back to Banchory.

6th Volunteer Battalion. "SOUTH AFRICA 1900-02"

The 6th Volunteer Battalion came from Banffshire, where a battalion was formed in 1861 to administer the County's three companies of rifle volunteers, each formed the previous year. Between 1863-1868 three more companies were added. In 1880 the Battalion was consolidated as 1st Corps, its headquarters being placed at Keith and its six companies located — Banff, Aberlour, Keith, Buckie, Minmore and Dufftown. A new company was added at Aberchirder in 1899.

7th Volunteer Battalion.

The 7th Volunteer Battalion was formed with an establishment of three companies in Shetland in 1900. Its headquarters were at Lerwick and the three companies located — Lerwick (2) and Scalloway. For administration purposes, the Shetlanders were attached to the 1st Volunteer Battalion.

Uniform

Both the 1st and 2nd Volunteer Battalions wore scarlet doublets, with yellow facings, and Gordon tartan trews,tThe 1st adopting the kilt after 1895. In the 3rd Volunteer Battalion a rifle green uniform, with scarlet facings, was worn up to 1883 when Gordon tartan trews were introduced. Two years later, scarlet doublets with yellow facings replaced the tunics and in 1903 kilts were substituted for the trews. The 4th Volunteer Battalion changed from a green tunic and trousers (scarlet facings) to rifle green doublet and Gordon tartan trews in 1887. Sixteen years later, the doublet was abolished and replaced by a drab service pattern, while at the same time kilts were introduced. A green doublet worn with Gordon tartan kilts was the uniform of the 5th Volunteer Battalion, and in 1891 the grey with black facings tunics and tousers of the 6th were replaced by scarlet doublets (yellow facings) and Gordon trews. A drab service dress was worn from formation by the 7th Volunteer Battalion.

Territorial Force
The reorganisations of 1908 saw the 1st Volunteer Battalion as 4th Battalion (TF), the 2nd and 3rd amalgamated as 5th, the 4th and 6th as 6th and the 5th as 7th Battalion. The 7th Volunteer Battalion appeared in the Army List as The Shetland Companies, The Gordon Highlanders.

59. 1st (Inverness Highland) Volunteer Battalion, Cameron Highlanders c1887. (Queen's Own Highlanders Regimental Museum).

QUEEN'S OWN CAMERON HIGHLANDERS

When the Cameron Highlanders were organised in 1881 it was the smallest infantry regiment in the British Army; there being only one line battalion (late 79th Foot), one militia battalion (late Highland Light Infantry Militia), and no volunteers. The Regiment was not enlarged until 1883, when its only volunteer battalion was added, and then in 1897, when a 2nd regular battalion was raised.

1st (Inverness Highland) Volunteer Battalion.
"SOUTH AFRICA 1900-02"

Ten numbered rifle corps were formed within the County of Inverness-shire during the first ten years of the Volunteer Movement. These were all placed into an administrative battalion, formed in 1860, and then in 1880 this was consolidated as 1st Inverness-shire Rifle Volunteer Corps.

From 1873 the Inverness-shire Rifle Volunteers had formed part of Number 55 Sub-District, and as such were linked to the 71st and 78th Regiments of Foot. In 1881 the 78th became the 2nd Battalion, Seaforth Highlanders, while at the same time the volunteers were allotted to that regiment. In 1883, however, the Corps was transferred to the Cameron Highlanders and in 1887 assumed the title — 1st (Inverness Highland) Volunteer Battalion.

The Battalion had its headquarters in Inverness and maintained an establishment of ten companies located as follows:- Inverness (4), Fort William, Kingussie, Beauly, Portree, Campbelltown and Roy Bridge, the latter moving to Fort Augustus in 1903.

Uniform

In 1863 the 1st Admin. Battalion of Inverness-shire Rifle Volunteers adopted Elcho Grey uniforms with green facings. Permission to change to scarlet doublets came in 1880 and at this time the facings became buff and the tartan — 42nd pattern. The next change was in 1893 when the uniform of the Cameron Highlanders (scarlet/blue, Cameron of Erracht tartan) was taken into use.

Territorial Force

The Battalion transferred in 1908 as the Regiment's 4th Battalion (TF).

60. Lieutenant, 1st (Renfrewshire) Volunteer Battalion, Princess Louise's (Argyll and Sutherland Highlanders). (Army Museums Ogilby Trust)

PRINCESS LOUISE'S (ARGYLL AND SUTHERLAND HIGHLANDERS)

The Regiment was at first known as Princess Louise's (Sutherland and Argyll Highlanders), but this title was changed to that shown above in 1882. With two line, two militia and seven volunteer battalions, the Regiment was formed — 1st Battalion (late 91st Foot), 2nd Battalion (late 93rd Foot), 4th Battalion (late Highland Borderers Militia), 4th Battalion (late Royal Renfrew Militia) and the volunteer corps of Argyllshire, Dumbartonshire, Renfrewshire, Stirlingshire and Clackmannan & Kinross. All but the 1st Dumbartonshire Rifle Volunteer Corps assumed the title of the Regiment in 1887.

1st (Renfrewshire) Volunteer Battalion.
"SOUTH AFRICA 1900-02"
The Battalion originated at Greenock in 1859, serving as the 1st Administrative Battalion of Renfrewshire Rifle Volunteers until 1880, and then as the County's 1st Corps. At first there were nine companies — Greenock (6), Port Glasgow, Gourock and Rothesay in Bute. In 1900 a new cyclist company was added, but six years later the Rothesay Company was closed down.

2nd (Renfrewshire) Volunteer Battalion.
"SOUTH AFRICA 1900-02"
The 2nd Administrative Battalion of Renfrewshire Rifle Volunteers was formed at Paisley in 1860, and in 1880 was consolidated as 2nd Corps with eight companies — Paisley (4), Johnstone, Kilbarchan, Lochwinnoch and Renfrew. In 1884 a new company was formed at Paisley, followed in 1900 by another consisting entirely of cyclists. Headquarters of "F" Company were moved from Lochwinnoch to Elderslie in 1903 and that same year "E" (Kilbarchan) Company was disbanded.

3rd (Renfrewshire) Volunteer Battalion.
"SOUTH AFRICA 1901-02"
Previously the 3rd Renfrewshire Rifle Volunteer Corps, and before that, the County's 3rd Administrative Battalion, the 3rd Volunteer Battalion was originally organised — Headquarters at Barrhead and eight companies located at Pollockshaws, Barrhead (2), Neilston, Thornliebank (2), Hurlet (later Newton-Mearns) and Cathcart. In 1881 headquarters of the Battalion were moved to Pollockshaws and in 1900 two new companies were raised at Barrhead, one, however, was disbanded in 1903.

4th (Stirlingshire) Volunteer Battalion.
"SOUTH AFRICA 1900-02"

In 1880 the 1st Administrative Battalion of Stirlingshire Rifle Volunteers was consolidated as the County's 1st Corps. Companies dated from 1859/60, and these were originally located at Stirling (3), Falkirk, Lennox Mill, Lennoxtown, Denny, Bannockburn, Carron and Kilsyth. Headquarters of the Battalion were in Stirling. Before 1908 the following reorganisations within the Battalion took place:- in 1880 the Lennox Mill Company ("D") moved to Falkirk and in 1904 "H" and "I" at Bannockburn and Carron were transferred to Stenhousemuir. Two years later the Stirling Company ("F") went to Falkirk.

5th Volunteer Battalion. "SOUTH AFRICA 1900-02"

Prior to 1887 the Battalion was the 1st Argyllshire Rifle Volunteer Corps, and before that, the County's 1st Administrative Battalion. Headquarters were at Dunoon and the Battalion's original eight companies, the senior dating from 1860, were located at Inveraray, Campbeltown (2), Dunoon, Glendaruel, Ballachulish (2) and Kilmartin. In 1882 the headquarters of "G" Company moved from Ballachulish to Southend just outside of Campbeltown. Then, in 1900, sanction to raise an additional two companies was granted and that year these were formed at Carradale and Campbeltown.

1st Dumbartonshire Volunteer Rifle Corps.
"SOUTH AFRICA 1900-02"

This corps, which ranked as 6th Volunteer Battalion and the only one in the Regiment not to assume its title, dates from 1860. After formation into an administrative battalion, the several corps within the County of Dumbartonshire were, in 1880, consolidated as 1st Corps. At this time headquarters were at Helensburgh and a twelve company establishment was located at Helensburgh, Cardross, Dumbarton, Bonhill, Jamestown, Alexandria, Clydebank, Maryhill, Milngavie, Kirkintilloch, Cumbernauld and Luss.

Before 1908 the following reorganisations took place within the Battalion: in 1882 the Luss Company was disbanded and replaced by one at Renton; 1884 saw the Cumbernauld personnel absorbed into Kirkintilloch and their place taken by a new company at Yorker. In 1900 two new companies were added, Maryhill forming a mounted infantry company while Dumbarton found one trained as cyclists.

7th (Clackmannan and Kinross) Volunteer Battalion.
"SOUTH AFRICA 1901-02"

This battalion was prior to 1887 the 1st Clackmannan and Kinross Rifle Volunteer Corps, and before 1880 the 1st

Administrative Battalion of Clackmannanshire. Save for the addition of a new company at Clackmannan in 1883, the organisation of the Battalion remained the same up to 1908 — Headquarters Alloa and seven companies located at Alloa (2), Sauchie, Dollar, Tillcoultry, Alva and Kinross.

Uniform
All volunteer battalions adopted, at different times, the scarlet doublets, yellow facings and Sutherland tartan of the Argyll and Sutherland Highlanders — 1st (grey/scarlet) in 1889, 2nd (scarlet/blue) in 1898, 3rd (scarlet/blue) in 1889, 4th (rifle-green/scarlet, Graham tartan, facings changing to rifle-green in 1882) in 1886, 5th (Argyll (Cawdor) Campbell tartan) in 1883, 1st Dumbarton (rifle-green/scarlet) in 1887 and 7th (scarlet/blue, Murray tartan) in 1888.

Territorial Force
In 1908 the transfer to the Territorial Force went as follows:- 1st V.B. became 5th Battalion, 2nd V.B. and 3rd V.B. amalgamated to form the 6th Battalion, 4th V.B. and 7th V.B. amalgamated as 7th Battalion, 5th V.B. became 8th Battalion and the 1st Dumbartons became 9th Battalion.

RIFLE BRIGADE (THE PRINCE CONSORT'S OWN)

In 1881 the Rifle Brigade comprised 1st to 4th (Regular) Battalions, 5th Battalion (late Queen's Own Royal Tower Hamlets Militia), 6th Battalion (late Royal Longford Militia), 7th Battalion (late King's Own Royal Tower Hamlets Militia), 8th Battalion (late Leitrim Militia) and 9th Battalion (late Westmeath Militia). The volunteers were provided by Middlesex and two Tower Hamlets corps.

7th Middlesex (London Scottish) Volunteer Rifle Corps. "SOUTH AFRICA 1900-02"
The 15th Middlesex Rifle Volunteer Corps was formed in 1859 by Scotsmen living in the London area. With eight companies the Corps was renumbered as 7th in 1880 and four years later increased its establishment to ten companies. Headquarters were in Adam Street, Adelphi until 1886 when a move was made to new premises at Buckingham Gate in South West London.

14th Middlesex (Inns of Court) Volunteer Rifle Corps. "SOUTH AFRICA 1900-01"
Formed as 23rd Middlesex at Lincoln's Inn in 1860 and

61. Bugler, 14th Middlesex (Inns of Court) Volunteer Rifle Corps. (Army Museums Ogilby Trust)

renumbered 14th in 1880. The Battalion at first comprised eight companies, but later maintained five infantry companies, a mounted infantry company and from 1900 one cyclist company.

15th Middlesex (The Customs and the Docks) Volunteer Rifle Corps.
"SOUTH AFRICA 1900-01"
Formed at Custom House in 1860, the 26th Middlesex was renumbered 15th in 1880. The original establishment was thirteen companies, but by 1891 this had been reduced to eight.

16th Middlesex (London Irish) Volunteer Rifle Corps.
"SOUTH AFRICA 1900-02"
Formed in 1860 as 28th Middlesex and renumbered as 16th in 1880. The London Irish maintained an establishment of twelve companies, its headquarters moving from 27 King William Street to 2 Duke Street, Charing Cross in 1897.

18th Middlesex Volunteer Rifle Corps.
"SOUTH AFRICA 1900-02"
Known locally as the "Paddington Rifles" the Battalion was formed as 36th Middlesex in 1860 and renumbered 18th with twelve companies in 1880. the 18th Middlesex was later reduced to ten, and finally eight companies.

19th Middlesex (St Giles's & St George's, Bloomsbury) Volunteer Rifle Corps.
"SOUTH AFRICA 1900-02"
Formed in 1860 as 37th Middlesex and renumbered 19th in 1880. The Battalion comprised ten companies.

20th Middlesex (Artists') Volunteer Rifle Corps.
"SOUTH AFRICA 1900-01"
Formed in 1860 as 38th Middlesex and renumbered 20th in 1880. The Battalion's eight companies were increased to twelve during the war in South Africa and its headquarters moved from 36 Fitzroy Square to Duke Street, Euston in 1888.

21st Middlesex (The Finsbury Rifle Volunteer Corps) Rifle Volunteer Corps.
Served as a volunteer battalion of the Rifle Brigade until transfer to the King's Royal Rifle Corps in 1883.

24th Middlesex Rifle Volunteer Corps.
"SOUTH AFRICA 1899-1902"
Formed as 49th Middlesex at Post Office Headquarters in London in 1868 and renumbered 24th in 1880. This battalion comprised ten, later twelve companies and was responsible for the formation in 1882 of the Army Postal Corps and in 1884 of the Field Telegraph Corps. The 24th also gained the honour "EGYPT 1882" but this is not shown in the Army List until after 1908.

26th Middlesex (Cyclist) Volunteer Rifle Corps.
See King's Royal Rifle Corps.

1st Tower Hamlets (The Tower Hamlets Rifle Volunteer Brigade) Volunteer Rifle Corps.
Served as a volunteer battalion of the Rifle Brigade until transfer to the Royal Fusiliers in 1904.

2nd Tower Hamlets Volunteer Rifle Corps.
"SOUTH AFRICA 1900-02"
The 1st Administrative Battalion of Tower Hamlets Rifle Volunteers was formed in 1861 and consolidated as 2nd Corps in 1880. Recruited throughout the East End of London, the Battalion moved its headquarters from 237 Whitechapel Road to 66 Tredegar road, Bow in 1894. There were eleven companies and these were originally located at 31 Quaker Street, Shoreditch (4), 14 Cambridge Road, Mile End (4) and 95 Worship Street, Finsbury (3).

Uniform
Uniform and facing colours were — 7th Middx: Elcho grey/blue, 14th Middx: grey/scarlet, 15th Middx: green/scarlet, 16th Middx: green/light green, 18th Middx: green/black, 19th Middx: green, 20th Middx: grey, 24th Middx: grey/blue then green/blue (Army List indicates change made in 1887), 2nd Tower Hamlets: grey/scarlet.

Territorial Force
The 14th Middlesex became the Inns of Court Officers Training Corps. All other corps became battalions of the London Regiment — 7th Middx. (14th Bn.), 15th Middx. (part of 17th Bn.), 16th Middx. (18th Bn.), 18th Middx. (10th Bn.), 19th Middx. (part of 9th Bn.), 20th Middx. (28th Bn.), 24th Middx. (8th Bn.), 2nd Tower Hamlets (part of 17th Bn.).